**Religions o**

Series Editor

G000241663

# JAPANESE
## RELIGIONS

**Michiko Yusa**

Western Washington University

London and New York

First published in Great Britain 2002
by Routledge
11 New Fetter Lane, London EC4P 4EE

*Routledge is an imprint of the Taylor & Francis Group*

Copyright © 2002 Laurence King Publishing Ltd

British Library Cataloguing in Publication Data
A catalogue record for this book is available from the British Library

ISBN 0-415-26284-4

This book was designed and produced by
LAURENCE KING PUBLISHING LTD, London
www.laurenceking.co.uk

*Editorial work* by Christine Davis, Richard Mason, Eleanor Van Zandt
*Design and artworks* by Karen Stafford
*Map* by Andrea Fairbrass
*Picture research* by Julia Ruxton
Printed in Hong Kong

*Reviewers* Livia Kohn, Boston University; Jane Marie Law, Cornell University; Mark MacWilliams, St. Lawrence University; Richard Pilgrim, Syracuse University; James Robinson, University of Northern Iowa

# Contents

# 7  The Modern Period  92

# 8 Japanese Religions in the New Millennium  109

# Foreword

## Religions of the World

The informed citizen or student needs a good overall knowledge of our small but complicated world. Fifty years ago you might have neglected religions. Now, however, we are shrewder and can see that religions and ideologies not only form civilizations but directly influence international events. These brief books provide succinct, balanced, and informative guides to the major faiths and one volume also introduces the changing religious scene as we enter the new millennium.

Today we want not only to be informed, but to be stimulated by the life and beliefs of the diverse and often complex religions of today's world. These insightful and accessible introductions allow you to explore the riches of each tradition – to understand its history, its beliefs and practices, and also to grasp its influence upon the modern world. The books have been written by a team of excellent and, on the whole, younger scholars who represent a new generation of writers in the field of religious studies. While aware of the political and historical influences of religion these authors aim to present the religion's spiritual side in a fresh and interesting way. So whether you are interested simply in descriptive knowledge of a faith, or in exploring its spiritual message, you will find these introductions invaluable.

The emphasis in these books is on the modern period, because every religious tradition has transformed itself in the face of the traumatic experiences of the last two hundred years or more. Colonialism, industrialization, nationalism, revivals of religion, new religions, world wars, revolutions, and social transformations have not left faith unaffected and have drawn on religious and anti-religious forces to reshape our world. Modern technology in the last 25 years—from the Boeing 747 to the world wide web—has made our globe seem a much smaller place. Even the moon's magic has been captured by technology.

We meet in these books people of the modern period as a sample of the many changes over the last few centuries. At the same time, each book provides a valuable insight into the different dimensions of the religion: its teachings, narratives, organizations, rituals, and experiences. In touching on these features, each volume gives a rounded view of the tradition enabling you to understand what it means to belong to a particular faith. As the native American proverb has it: "Never judge a person without walking a mile in his moccasins."

To assist you further in your exploration, a number of useful reference aids are included. Each book contains a chronology, map, glossary, pronunciation guide, list of festivals, annotated reading list, and index. A selection of images provide examples of religious art, symbols, and contemporary practices. Focus boxes explore in more detail the relation between the faith and some aspect of the arts—whether painting, sculpture, architecture, literature, dance or music.

I hope you will find these introductions enjoyable and illuminating. Brevity is supposed to be the soul of wit: it can also turn out to be what we need in the first instance in introducing cultural and spiritual themes.

*Ninian Smart*
*Santa Barbara, 1998*

# Preface

In today's increasingly interdependent world, it is vitally important that different nations and cultures understand one another. Many Westerners have acquired some understanding of Japan—through contact with visiting Japanese students, perhaps, or even through travel to Japan. Even so, Japan tends to be seen predominantly in its modern role, as a key player in the global economy; the nation's distinctive humanistic traditions are often overlooked. Japanese culture is a complex amalgam of old and new, and because Japan's various religions have been central to the development of this culture, they serve as windows to the Japanese people's sense of identity.

In the following pages I have adopted a chronological approach to the study of Japanese religions. I have placed religious events, experiences, and customs in a framework of Japanese history, which includes an account of Japan's interactions with the Western world. It is hoped that this small book will serve as a useful guide to the spiritual traditions of the Japanese people.

In the summer of 2000, I made extensive pilgrimages to sacred places in Japan in preparation for the writing of this book. I would like to thank Professor A. Mineshima, who kindly guided me through Zojoji in Tokyo, the head temple of the Pure Land sect. I would also like to thank Professor Z. Hidaka, abbot of the Sanboin temple at Mt. Koya. Although I did not write about the religion of the Ainu people, I learned much about them from meeting with Dr. S. Kayano at the village of Nibutani, in Hokkaido.

Moreover, I am deeply indebted to the work of Japanese scholars such as Kanaoka Shuyu, Ishida Mizumaro, Miyasaki Yusho, Kino Kazuyoshi, Nakamura Hijime, Murakami Shigeyoshi, Tamura Encho, and many others.

My special thanks go to Professor Edward Kaplan, my colleague at Western Washington University, who read my earlier drafts and made expert editorial comments. My thanks go also to Melanie White, Richard Mason, Kate Tuckett, Eleanor Van Zandt, and Julia Ruxton, of Laurence King Publishing Ltd., whose tireless encouragement was essential for the completion of this book. I owe special thanks to Christine Davis, Project Editor, as well as to the reviewers whose comments were of invaluable assistance. I thank Western Washington University for its Faculty Development Grant.

I will never know what Professor Ninian Smart would have had to say about this book, but I hope that I would not have disappointed him. I dedicate this small but dear book to Ninian and his beloved wife, Libushka, with all my love.

*Michiko Yusa*
*September 2001*

# Timeline

| Period* | Religion | Japanese History | World History |
|---|---|---|---|
| **Jōmon** 11,000?–300 B.C.E. | • Animism, belief in all sorts of spirits | • Period of hunting, fishing, and gathering | • Socrates, Plato, Aristotle, Gautama Buddha, Confucius |
| **Yayoi** c. 300 B.C.E.– c. 200 C.E. | • Belief in *kami* spirits established • Ancestor worship spreads | • Japan divided into tribal states | • Mencius, Jesus of Nazareth • 202 B.C.E.–220 C.E. Han dynasty (China) |
| **Yamato** (or "Tumuli") c. 200–c. 500 | • Erection of first Shinto shrines • Confucianism and Daoism introduced by Korean and Chinese émigrés | • Queen Himiko (r. c. 180–248) • Unification of Japan by the imperial family | • 313 Christianity officially recognized in Roman Empire |
| **Asuka** c. 500–645 | • 538 Introduction of Buddhism from Paekche • Prince Shotoku patronizes Buddhism | • Consolidation of imperial rule • System of bureaucracy modeled after China introduced | • 589–618 Sui dynasty (China) • 622 Muhammad's *hijirah*, the emigration of the Prophet (Islam) |
| **Hakuhō** 645–710 | • Shinto and Buddhism coexist amicably | • Emperor Tenmu orders compilation of the early history of Japan | • 618–907 Tang dynasty (China) |
| **Nara** 710–784 | • Nara Buddhist schools flourish • 752 Dedication of the Great Buddha Image at Tōdaiji | • The country is centralized under the rule of the imperial family | • c. 700 Celtic, Roman missionaries convert Anglo-Saxons (England) • 717 Saracens besiege Constantinople |
| **Heian** 794–1192 | • Founding of Tendai sect at Mt. Hiei and Shingon sect at Mt. Koya • 1052 Beginning of *mappo*, the "period of the decline of Buddha's teaching" • Faith in Amida's Paradise and the practice of *nenbutsu* spreads | • Aristocrats (esp. the Fujiwara family) dominate the imperial court • Rise of warriors to power • 1185 Defeat of the Taira clan by the Minamoto clan | • 960–1279 Song dynasty (China) • 988 Russian Orthodox Church established • 1054 Split of the Christian church into Greek Orthodox and Roman Catholic • 1066 Norman conquest of England • 1096–1270 Crusades • 1130–1200 Zhu Xi (China) |

Gaps in the dates in this list indicate transitional periods. These names and the period dates vary slightly from one source to another.

| Kamakura 1192–1333 | • Period of great religious leaders: Honen, Shinran, Eisai, Dogen, Nichiren, and Ippen (rise of "Kamakura Buddhism") • Chinese Chan masters emigrate to Japan • Articulation of Shinto as a religion begins | • 1192 Minamoto Yoritomo establishes the shogunate in Kamakura • The Hojo regent seizes political power • 1274 and 1281: Mongol invasions | • 1215 Magna Carta signed • 1260 Khubilai Khan enthroned as leader of the Mongols • 1271–1368 Yuan dynasty (China) • 1271–95 Marco Polo in China |
|---|---|---|---|
| Muromachi 1336–1573 | • Spread of idea of Japan as a divinely protected country • Development of "Kamakura Buddhist" sects • Zen Buddhism pervades the arts | • 1336–92 Imperial court is divided into northern and southern courts • 1338 Ashikaga Takauji establishes the shogunate in Kyoto | • 1368–1644 Ming dynasty (China) • The Renaissance • Exploration of ocean routes • 1492 Columbus's "discovery" of the Americas; fall of Moorish Granada |
| [Sengoku] (Warring States Period) c. 1460–1573 | • Militant religious communities develop • 1536 Attack on Nichiren temples in Kyoto • 1549 Francis Xavier introduces Christianity • 1571 Oda Nobunaga attacks Mt. Hiei | • 1467–1477 Onin War • Japan plunges into volatile period of civil war among warlords | • 1472–1529 Wan Yangming (China) • 1517 Reformation begins • 1534 Church of England established • 1545–63 Catholic Counter-Reformation |
| Azuchi-Momoyama 1573–1603 | • 1587 First prohibition of Christianity | • 1573 Oda Nobunaga seizes Kyoto • 1582 Toyotomi Hideyoshi succeeds Nobunaga | • Queen Elizabeth I (r. 1558–1603) • 1577–80 Sir Francis Drake circumnavigates globe • 1598 Edict of Nantes |
| Edo (or Tokugawa) 1603–1867 | • Persecution of Christians • Blossoming of Confucian learning and other ethical schools • Studies of ancient Japanese literature emerge • 19th century: burgeoning of popular religious movements | • 1603 Tokugawa Ieyasu establishes the shogunate in Edo (Tokyo) • 1639 Closure of ports • 1854 U.S.–Japan treaty signed • 1858 Opening of ports to Western countries | • 1644–1912 Qing dynasty (China) • c. 1770 Industrial revolution begins in Britain • 1776 Thirteen colonies in America declare independence from Britain • 1789 French Revolution |
| Meiji 1868–1912 | • Shinto chosen as national faith • 1868 Separation of Shinto and Buddhism • 1873 Ban on Christianity lifted • Buddhist and other spiritual movements flourish | • 1868 Meiji Restoration • 1889 Promulgation of Meiji Constitution • 1894–95 Sino–Japanese War • 1904–5 Russo–Japanese War | • Queen Victoria (r. 1837–1901) • 1869 Suez Canal opens • 1893 World Parliament of Religions in Chicago |

| | | | |
|---|---|---|---|
| **Taishō**<br>**1912–1926** | • Marxist ideology becomes popular among intellectuals; suppressed by government | • Brief flowering of democracy | • 1914–18 World War I<br>• 1914 Panama Canal opens<br>• 1917 Russian Revolution |
| **Shōwa**<br>**1926–1989** | • State Shinto elevated to national faith<br>• Soka Gakkai, Reiyukai, Rissho Koseikai, and other popular sects emerge<br>• Postwar dismantling of State Shinto<br>• 1945–50s Rise of "new religions" | • 1930s Rise of ultranationalist sentiments<br>• 1945 Atomic bombs dropped on Hiroshima and Nagasaki<br>• 1945–52 Allied forces occupy Japan<br>• 1960s Rapid urbanization, economic recovery, technological advancement | • 1939–45 World War II<br>• 1949 People's Republic of China established<br>• 1950–53 Korean War<br>• 1954–75 Vietnam War |
| **Heisei**<br>**1989–present** | • 1995 Sarin gas attack on Tokyo subway by Aum Shinrikyo members | • 1980s Economic boom<br>• 1990s Slump followed by sluggish economic recovery<br>• Emergence of political conservatism<br>• Juvenile crime rate climbs up | • 1989 Fall of the Berlin Wall<br>• 2001 The Taliban destroy ancient Buddhist statues at Bamiyan in Afghanistan |

MAP OF JAPAN

0 ⊢ 200 miles
0 ⊢ 300 km

N

HOKKAIDO
Sapporo
• Hakodate

• Aomori
• Akita

Sado Island

• Niigata    • Sendai

Nikko

Kanazawa
Izumo   Mt. Hiei    HONSHU
Yamaguchi

Dazaifu    Hiroshima   Kyoto  Nara   Mt. Fuji   Edo / Tokyo
                      Osaka • Ise
Nagasaki              Kumano    Kamakura
KYUSHU    SHIKOKU   Mt. Koya
Kagoshima

PACIFIC OCEAN

<table>
<tr><td>Japanese Religions, Past and Present</td><td>1</td></tr>
</table>

# Japanese Religions, Past and Present — 1

## A Chronological Framework

The religion of any people develops over time; and so it has been for the Japanese. To understand Japanese religion today, it is important to have a historical knowledge of, for instance, how Buddhism was introduced into Japan, how it interacted with the native Shinto tradition, and how, together with Shinto, it fundamentally shaped the subsequent Japanese religious landscape. Over the centuries, new ideas, ritual practices, and beliefs have emerged; some have then disappeared, while others, some quite ancient, have persisted to this day. A chronological approach to Japanese religions, as used in this book, will trace—and, it is hoped, illuminate—these developments.

### Japanese Historical Periods and Religions—A Brief Overview

Japanese history is divided into "periods," which are named according to various criteria. For example, the Jomon (c. 11,000? B.C.E.–c. 300 B.C.E.) and Yayoi (c. 300 B.C.E.–c. 200 C.E.) periods are distinguished by major technological shifts, as evidenced by their styles of pottery and earthenware. While "Jomon" refers to the "rope pattern" found on the pottery of that period, "Yayoi" is the name of an excavation site in Tokyo where a newer type of pottery, made with the use of a potter's wheel, was discovered. This technological shift is attributed to the arrival of a new culture to Japan from the Chinese mainland and the Korean peninsula. The Yamato period (c. 200 C.E.–c. 500 C.E.) takes its name from the region where the most powerful clan ruled. This clan eventually subdued other clans and became Japan's imperial family. An alternative name for this period, Kofun (tumuli), refers to the large burial mounds of the clan chiefs.

Archaeological digs and discoveries continually alter our picture of early Japanese history, calling into question many of our assumptions about the lives and religious practices of ancient peoples. Critical scholarship will no doubt eventually unravel many of the mysteries, but for the time being we must make do with referring to the oldest extant written texts, by the Chinese, as well as to Japanese accounts of the country's early history, the **Records of Ancient Matters** (*Kojiki,* compilation completed in 712 C.E.) and the **Chronicles of Japan** (*Nihongi,* compilation completed in 720 C.E.). Generally speaking, however, it is conjectured that during the Jomon period animistic beliefs prevailed, and that during the Yayoi period the practice of ancestor worship was established. The worship of **kami** (spirits of nature, clan deities, or gods), the practice of ritual purification, and the use of divination and oracles delivered by the shamanic mediums were all prominent features of early Shinto practice.

The Asuka period (c. 500–c. 645), named after the geographic area of an early capital, saw increased contact with Korea and China. A large number of Koreans emigrated to Japan, bringing with them advanced continental learning and skills, including architecture, engineering techniques, the calendar system, and classical Chinese learning (**Confucian, Daoist,** and Legalist texts). Buddhism, too, was introduced from Korea in 538 C.E. and soon received royal patronage.

Through the Taika Reform of 645, the imperial family established a centralized form of government by adopting the Chinese legal system (*ritsuryo*). This period is known as the Hakuho period (c. 645–710), a name drawn from art history. Much enamored with the advanced Chinese culture of the Tang dynasty (618–907), Japanese leaders eagerly absorbed it, and art and literature blossomed. Buddhism gained a solid foothold during this time, while major Shinto shrines also received imperial patronage.

The centralization of political power by the imperial family was reflected in the construction of a new capital, Nara, after which the following period (710–784) is named. The city was modeled on the Tang capital, Chang'an. Nara—also known as Heijoko, "the capital of peaceful palace"—was adorned with magnificent Buddhist monasteries and nunneries. The Great Buddha image of the Todaiji temple symbolized the height of glory accorded to Buddhism.

In 784 the imperial court left Nara and ten years later established a new capital, Heiankyo ("peaceful capital"), in Kyoto. In the early days of the Heian period (794–1192), two Buddhist monasteries were established: at Mt. Hiei (the **Tendai** sect) and at Mt. Koya (the **Shingon** sect). These sects flourished thanks to the patronage of the imperial court and its courtiers. From the mid-Heian period onward, a general sense of instability prevailed and people turned to Buddhism for salvation and especially embraced **Amida Buddha**. Also by the middle of this period a class of *samurai* (warriors) had grown out of the provincial guards. Power struggles among the aristocrats developed over time into military conflicts, involving the two most prominent military families—the Taira (or Heike) and the Minamoto (or Genji). With the defeat of the Taira family, the courtiers lost their political hold.

In 1192, the head of the Minamoto family, Yoritomo (1147–99), was granted the title of *shogun* (generalissimo) by the imperial court and established a military government (the shogunate) in Kamakura, after which this period (1192–1333) is named. After the death of Yoritomo, his wife, Masako, and her father, regent Hojo Tokimasa, seized political power and controlled the shogunate from the office of regent. New Buddhist sects arose during this period, the prominent ones being the **Pure Land**, the **True Pure Land**, the **Zen**, and the **Nichiren** sects.

On the Chinese continent, Khubilai Khan (1215–94), the anointed leader of the Mongols, had established the Yuan dynasty in 1271 and annihilated the southern Song court in 1279. Twice, in 1274 and 1281, the Mongol army attempted to invade Japan to subjugate it, but without success, due to the opportune typhoon winds. The seemingly miraculous deliverance from this formidable threat gave rise to the idea among the Japanese that the typhoon winds were sent by gods and thus divine (*kamikaze*), befitting the land ruled by the descendants of gods (*shinkoku*).

In 1333, the emperor Godaigo (r. 1318–39), wishing to regain political power from the shogunate, launched a *coup*, and thanks to the military strategy of Ashikaga Takauji (1305–58) he defeated the Hojo regent. Takauji, however, coveted the title of shogun, and in 1336 he turned against Godaigo and enthroned a new emperor in his place. The deposed emperor fled to Yoshino, taking the **three imperial regalia** with him, and established his own court in the south. For some time Japan had two emperors; this is known as the period of southern and northern courts (1336–92). Takauji was appointed shogun in 1338 and established his shogunate in the Muromachi ward of Kyoto, after which the Muromachi period (1336–1573) is named. Following Takauji's example, many Ashikaga shoguns patronized Zen Buddhism, and the Zen-inspired culture flourished. By this time, Buddhist sects that had arisen during the Kamakura period were also increasingly popular.

The Ashikaga shogunate was plagued by power struggles from within and among its regents, and following the Onin War of 1467–77, which devastated Kyoto, the shogunate's power severely declined and the country fell into disunity. Along with the decline of the shogunate's resources came the impoverishment of the imperial family. During this time, the periodic rebuilding of the Ise Shrine (see Chapter 2) was suspended. The second half of the Muromachi period is better known as the Sengoku ("warring states") period; the country was divided into territories occupied by warlords (*daimyo*), vying to gain control of Japan. Although this was a period of continual, often ferocious fighting, it was also a dynamic period, when opportunities were abundant for anyone with military talent. It was into this war-torn Japan that Christianity was introduced in 1549 by Francis Xavier.

When Oda Nobunaga (1534–82) emerged victorious among the warlords and entered Kyoto in 1573, the last Ashikaga shogun resigned, thus ending the Muromachi period. After Nobunaga was assassinated, his general, Toyotomi Hideyoshi (1538–98), continued the military campaign to unify Japan, proving successful in 1590. This period, ruled by the heroic military leaders, is known as the Azuchi-Momoyama period (1573–1603) after the locations of two majestic castles built by Nobunaga and Hideyoshi, respectively. Nobunaga patronized Christianity, which he saw could curtail the political power of Buddhism. Hideyoshi's reaction to Christianity was ambivalent, initially favorable but later suspicious.

Following the death of Hideyoshi in 1598, an ally, Tokugawa Ieyasu (1542–1616), seized power. Appointed shogun by the emperor in 1603, Ieyasu established the shogunate in Edo (modern Tokyo). During the Edo (or Tokugawa) period (1603–1867), the shogunate imposed numerous restrictions on the lives of the people in order to maintain a rigid feudal social system. It also closed off almost all Japanese ports to Western countries. Christianity was prohibited, and Buddhism gained the status of a quasi-national religion. While Neo-Confucian learning thrived, nationalistic interpretations of Shinto also gained many adherents. During the early nineteenth century a number of popular religious sects sprang up.

In October 1867, the last Tokugawa shogun voluntarily abdicated, and in the following year, political power was transferred (or restored) to the emperor—an event known as the Meiji Restoration of 1868. It was decided then that one period name be given to each emperor's reign. During the Meiji period (1868–1912), which means "enlightened reign," the government strove to modernize Japan by emulating European and North American countries; it encouraged heavy industry and built up the military. Christianity was legalized during this time. In this spirit of radical departure from the past, the government attempted to establish Shinto as the national religion, by separating it from Buddhism. At a popular level, a renewed interest in spiritual quests prevailed.

On the death of the Meiji emperor Mutsuhito in 1912, Crown Prince Yoshihito ascended the throne, ushering in the Taisho period (1912–26), meaning "the reign through great rectitude." Western democracy briefly flourished and socialist movements spread. But the government was beset by financial difficulties, which eventually led to social turmoil. Lay Buddhist sects began to emerge around this time. In 1926, following the death of his father, Crown Prince Hirohito became emperor, and the period of his reign (1926–89) was named Showa, which stood for "domestic social stability and the cooperation of the countries abroad." During the 1930s, as military expansionism gained momentum, Shinto rites were elevated into the national religion of "State Shinto" (or *Kokka Shinto*).

Japan's defeat in World War II in 1945 was followed by the occupation under the Allied forces, which sought to dismantle State Shinto. Starting in the 1960s, Japan experienced rapid urbanization and a technological revolution, which created a spiritual vacuum. To fill this need, religious sects that had been formed in the 1920s and 1930s gained a large number of followers, and newer sects, too, appeared on the scene. In the 1970s and 1980s, another wave of new sects, dubbed "new-new religions," rose up. With the death of Emperor Hirohito on January 8, 1989, Crown Prince Akihito ascended the throne, launching the Heisei ("peace achieved") period.

## Some Features of Japanese Religions

Traditional Japanese religiosity is basically a mixture of Shinto and Buddhism, with other religious elements drawn from Confucianism, popular Daoism, and folk religions woven into the framework of Buddhist and Shinto practices.

The word "Shinto" is used in this book to refer not to any specific form of Shinto sect or credo but rather to the native Japanese religious practices and religious sentiments, ancient in origin and still found today in the deep recesses of the Japanese psyche as a sort of cultural and spiritual matrix. This "Shinto mentality" generally affirms the world and considers health, wealth, and happiness as signs of the protection of the *kami*—gods and other supernatural powers.

Japanese Buddhist sects are largely those of the **Mahayana** persuasion (see Chapter 3). Buddhism's message of universal salvation deepened people's spiritual awareness and sharpened their sense of morality. In time, Buddhism was "naturalized" to Japan, and together with Shinto it thoroughly shaped Japanese culture. For example, a word *dan'na*, the Japanese word for the head of the household, actually comes from **Sanskrit** *dāna*, "almsgiving" or "religious offering," via Buddhism.

Shinto and Buddhism have interacted in multitudinous ways, but at a popular level the two have achieved a comfortable "division of labor." Luis de Almeida, a Portuguese Jesuit who visited the Kasuga Shrine, in Nara, in May 1565, observed that "the Japanese pray to *kami* (deities) for longevity, health, wealth, fame, and all the other worldly benefits, while they turn to *hotoke* (Buddha) for their personal religious salvation."[1] Remarkably, this division has persisted in Japan to this day.

## Religions in Contemporary Japan

It is casually said that the Japanese are "born Shinto and die Buddhist." But some Japanese claim that they "die Shinto," because they draw comfort from the thought that they are joining their ancestors when they die. Be that as it may, for many Japanese, Shinto and Buddhism complement each other to the point that the boundary between them is hardly discernible. Most Japanese do not consciously distinguish between Shinto-related and Buddhism-related activities. Moreover, many ancient religious activities, such as the year-end general cleaning and numerous festivals, have long since become cultural activities that punctuate the lives of the people.

Until the move toward urbanization took hold in the 1960s, Japanese people were born into the religious faith of their families. However, with the breakdown of the extended family system into nuclear family units, religious faith progressively became a matter of individual choice. For this reason, it is not uncommon for a Japanese person to have more than one religious affiliation, something which would be unthinkable in strictly monotheistic cultures. This flexible attitude toward religion has made room for numerous new religious sects to mushroom in the postwar period.

While religious sentiments and needs are universal, what distinguishes the contemporary Japanese attitude toward religion is its downright affirmation of the world in which we live. Ideas of going to heaven or accruing religious merits are hardly motives for most people to do good; if the Japanese do good works, it is because they know that such acts will contribute to the general welfare of society. Religious ceremonies and practices are focused on the present—wishing for the benefit of individuals and the peace of the world.

## Art as Religion

Although religion and art enjoy a symbiotic relationship throughout the world, this interrelationship is especially pronounced in Japan. The reflective awareness that Buddhism cultivated among the Japanese, for instance, made possible such literary masterpieces as *The Tale of Genji*, which is imbued with a sense of gentle pathos, and *The Tale of the Heike*, which is filled with the Buddhist sense of the transience (*mujo*) of earthly existence.

The form of Japanese poetry, the *waka*, was closely associated with Shinto, because the literary gift was considered a blessing of the gods, and gifted poets of ancient times were often deified. In time, however, the mental concentration required to compose fine *waka* was felt to contain the elements of Buddhist meditation practices. For example, an influential poet of the late Heian period, Fujiwara no Shunzei (1114–1204), the father of the celebrated poet Teika, came to embrace the conviction that poetry making (*kado*) was identical with Buddhist practice (*butsudo*). Artistic, creative activities came to bear the stamp of religious practice.

Art forms that were developed during the medieval Kamakura and Muromachi periods, such as the tea ceremony, flower arrangement, and **noh** plays, all require diligent physical, mental, and spiritual discipline, reminiscent of arduous religious practices. As a result, artistic pursuits and appreciation came to be perceived as an alternative to spiritual salvation—a theme found in many popular Japanese religious sects today.

## "The Way of *Kami*"

Native Japanese religious practices acquired the name "Shinto" ("the way of *kami*") only to distinguish them from "the way of Buddha," once Buddhism was introduced into Japan in the sixth century C.E. Until then, there had obviously been no need to label the indigenous religious practices of the Japanese people.

The first appearance of the term "Shinto" is found in Book 21 ("Emperor Yomei" r. 585–87) of the *Nihongi*, or the *Chronicles of Japan*.[1]

The word "*kami*" has several meanings. It can refer to spirits of nature—mountains, rivers, trees, rocks, and ocean—all conceived to be alive and sacred. It may also refer to the deity dwelling in these natural objects, or indeed to a supernatural power, a collective ancestor spirit that protects a clan (the early Japanese social unit). The *kami* spirit may be incarnate in certain individuals—brave, unusual, or gifted—and these individuals may be deified as living *kami*. The *kami* may deliver its oracles through shamanic mediums, who were considered the "children of the spirit," or *miko*.

### The Sacred

The great scholar Motoori Norinaga (1730–1801) summarized the meanings of *kami* in these words:

> Speaking in general, it may be said that *kami* signifies, in
> the first place, the deities of heaven and earth that appear in
> the ancient records and also the *kami* spirits of the shrines
> where they are worshipped. It is hardly necessary to say
> that it includes human beings. It also includes such objects

as birds, beasts, trees, plants, seas, mountains, and so forth.
In ancient usage, anything whatsoever which was outside
the ordinary, which possessed superior power, or which was
awe-inspiring was called *kami*. Eminence here does not
refer merely to the superiority of nobility, goodness, or
meritorious deeds. Evil and mysterious things, if they are
extraordinary and dreadful, are called *kami*. It is needless to
say that among human beings who are called *kami* the
successive generations of sacred emperors are all included.[2]

The *kami* are not necessarily good; partaking of the ambigu-
ous nature of the "sacred," they can have both good and evil powers.
The tone of Motoori's description is reminiscent of the German scholar
of religion, Rudolf Otto's definition of the holy: *mysterium, tremen-
dum et fascinosum* ("mysterious, awe-inspiring, and fascinating").
The extraordinary, the awe-inspiring manifest themselves as creative
or destructive forces.

In fact, at the Ise Shrine, the goddess **Amaterasu**'s "wild spirit"
(*aratama*) is separately enshrined and worshipped, for with proper
worship a negative power may become beneficial. Implicit in this practice is an acknowledgment that the forces of nature are both constructive
and destructive, and that life entails harmony and conflict, peace and
war. The realm of extraordinary spirits is beyond human concepts
of morality.

## Early Shinto Practice

Although earthquakes, typhoons, and other natural calamities are
common occurrences, Japan's natural environment, both land and
sea, provides the people with rich sustenance. For the ancient Japanese, "life was good and beautiful; human beings had reason to be
thankful for their lot in this world."[3] Whatever occupation they engaged
in, be it farming, hunting, or handicrafts, they felt they were "instru-
ments of the *kami*, who worked through them."[4] While Shinto affirmed
this world, it also imposed taboos, which were strictly observed. Death,
blood, and sickness were major "pollutants," which people had to
avoid. Once a person came in contact with any of the multitude of
pollutants, he or she had to undergo a ritual purification, performed
by the clan priest. Such a purification ritual is mentioned in the record

of the Chinese kingdom of Wei (220–65 C.E.), in this case relating to funeral practices of the country of "Wa," as Japan was then known by the Chinese. A passage from the *History of the Kingdom of Wei* (compiled c. 297 C.E.) reads:

> When a person dies, they prepare a single coffin, without an outer one. They cover the graves with earth to make a mound. When death occurs, mourning is observed for more than ten days, during which period they do not eat meat. The head mourners wail and lament, while friends sing, dance, and drink liquor. When the funeral is over, all members of the family go into the water to cleanse themselves in a bath of purification.[5]

## Himiko, the Shamanic Queen

The *History of the Kingdom of Wei* also mentions a Japanese queen-sorceress, Himiko (variation Pimiko; r. c. 180–248 C.E). It reads:

> She occupied herself with magic and sorcery, bewitching the people. Though mature in age, she remained unmarried. She had a younger brother who assisted her in ruling the country. After she became the ruler, there were few who saw her. She had one thousand women as attendants, but only one man. He served her food and drink and acted as a medium of communication. She resided in a palace surrounded by towers and stockades, with armed guards in a state of constant vigilance.[6]

The account continues that Himiko sent an envoy to the court of the king of Wei in 238 C.E; after Himiko passed away, "a great mount was raised, more than a hundred paces in diameter. Over a hundred male and female attendants followed her to the grave."[7] A king ascended the throne, but the people would not obey him, and the country fell into chaos. Himiko's relative, Iyo, "a girl of thirteen, was then made queen and order was restored."[8]

What is curious is that this powerful queen, Himiko, is nowhere mentioned in the two earliest Japanese historical accounts—the *Records of Ancient Matters* and the *Chronicles of Japan*. Some have argued that the image of Himiko inspired the myth of the sun goddess Amaterasu.[9] The fact is that the Shinto myths that form the earliest section of these two historical records are open to all sorts of interpretations.[10]

Recent archaeological findings support the Chinese account that Himiko lived in the Yamato period rather than at the end of the Yayoi period. This naturally raises the question of whether the country of Wa was identical to the Yamato court of the imperial family. To this day, there is no conclusive evidence to substantiate or contradict this theory, and more archaeological facts need to be unearthed.

## The Sun Goddess Amaterasu in Shinto Myths

Myths surrounding the birth of the land of Japan, and stories of the sun goddess, have traditionally formed the basis of the political claim that sought to legitimize Japan's imperial line of succession from the "Age of Gods." For this reason it will be helpful to give here a brief overview of these Shinto myths, as compiled in the *Records of Ancient Matters* and the *Chronicles of Japan*.[11]

In the beginning, it is said, was chaos, amidst which a *kami* deity appeared, followed by several generations of single gods and a god and goddess as a couple. Although the ways of reckoning vary between the two sources, **Izanagi**, "the male who invites," and **Izanami**, "the female who invites," were the "seventh generation" of the *kami*,[12] and it was they who created the Japanese islands. The story goes that they looked down on the sea from the floating bridge of heaven and made the sea salt coagulate to create a small island, onto which they descended. Out of their act of procreation were born the islands of Japan, including mountains, rivers, trees, grasses, grains, animals, and minerals. When Izanami gave birth to a fire god, she was badly burned, died, and descended into the land of the dead. Her loving husband, Izanagi, missing her terribly, visited her in the underworld. She made him promise that if he did not look at her until they had escaped from the underworld, she would rejoin the living. Of course, curiosity overcame Izanagi. He looked at her and lo! he saw an ugly decomposing body. Ashamed of her ugliness, Izanami became angry, and turned on him and chased him. Izanagi narrowly escaped this horror and put a seal at the gate of the underworld. Having come in contact with the dead, which is a major defilement, Izanagi underwent a purification ritual in the river. When he washed his left eye, the sun goddess Amaterasu was born; from his nose, the wind god **Susanoo** was born; and when he washed his right eye, the moon god **Tsukiyomi** was born. These are the three "august children." Izanagi gave Amaterasu dominion over heaven, Susanoo dominion over the sea, and Tsukiyomi dominion over the night.

Susanoo was a wild child; he harbored a deep longing for his mother, Izanami, whom he had never seen. He insisted on seeing his mother, and finally Izanagi consented. Before going to the land of the dead to see her, however, Susanoo decided to visit his older sister, Amaterasu, in order to bid her farewell. Suspicious of Susanoo's intentions in coming to heaven, Amaterasu challenged him to prove his sincerity. The brother and the sister engaged in "jewel spitting" by taking jewels from each other's belongings (jewels were associated with fetuses). From each jewel spat, a child was born. Through this competition, Amaterasu gave birth to three daughters from Susanoo's jewels, and Susanoo gave birth to five sons from Amaterasu's jewels. Amaterasu declared that the three girls born out of Susanoo's sword were his, and the five boys born out of her earrings, hair ornaments, and necklace were hers. Susanoo reasoned that his jewels giving birth to "gentle females" proved his sincerity, and Amaterasu accepted this and allowed him to stay in her domain for a while.

Having won the confidence of his older sister, Susanoo became euphoric and gave free rein to his rambunctious nature. He broke the dike of his sister's rice paddy, which dried up the paddy and killed the rice plants. He then excreted on the floor of the sacred hall. Finally, he threw a skinned and bloody colt into a weaving chamber. A maiden weaver, shocked by the gruesome sight, jumped on a weaving needle, and fatally injured herself. Susanoo had thus interfered with the sacred duty of Amaterasu, to wear a new robe to dedicate the first harvest of the rice plants at the sacred altar—the central symbolic role of the emperor, which has carried on down to this day.

## The Incident of the "Heavenly Rock Cave" and the Imperial Regalia

Horrified by the death of her maiden servant, Amaterasu hid herself in the rock cavern, which plunged the earth into eternal night. The gods were troubled and gathered together to decide what to do. One wise *kami* reckoned that it would be best to entice Amaterasu out of the cavern by putting on a festival. So the gods dug up and transplanted a young sacred *sakaki* tree (where the divine spirit is believed to dwell) in front of the cave and hung sacred jewels from its branches. Likewise the gods braided a thick straw rope and also cast and polished a divine mirror to be used to entice Amaterasu out of the cave. They made a rooster crow in their hope for the arrival of the dawn. A goddess, Uzume, began dancing on a wooden tub turned upside down, so that whenever she stamped her foot, it made a loud reverberating sound. As she danced, Uzume was transported into a state of ecstasy; she exposed her nipples and tucked up her skirt so high as to reveal her private parts. (Her dance is a symbolic expression of the fertile mother earth.) The gathered deities broke into uproarious applause, clapping and shouting. Inside the cave, Amaterasu wondered why the deities were so delighted. She grew curious and slid aside the rock door just a bit to look outside. A deity put forth the polished mirror in front of her face, which reflected Amaterasu's beautiful countenance. Not realizing that she was looking at her own reflection, she was momentarily bewildered. Just then, a muscular god flung open the rock door and escorted her out of the cave. Another god put the braided rope across the cave, keeping Amaterasu from returning to it. The world became bright again. (Incidentally, goddess Uzume is considered the founding deity of the noh drama, whose essence is to bring delight—a pun on the word, meaning both enjoyment and "light"—to the audience.)

Amaterasu, now a reigning queen, took Takamimusubi, one of the older gods, as her political counselor, and together they ruled heaven. (There is a parallel story of how Himiko ruled her country with the help of her brother.) Susanoo was banished from heaven to the land of **Izumo**. There, he became a local hero after killing an eight-headed serpent and rescuing a maiden condemned to be a sacrificial offering to the serpent; he then took this maiden as his wife. Discovering a sword hidden in the tail of the serpent, he sent it to Amaterasu in heaven as a peace offering. Susanoo's descendants ruled far and wide in the Izumo region. The local deity of Izumo, Okuninushi, was a powerful god, endowed with the quality of a medicine man, and Susanoo came to be closely associated with him in the myth. The shrine at Izumo (Izumo Taisha) was erected for Okuninushi. It has long been known for its matchmaking efficacy; and even today, those who wish to find a marriage partner visit the great shrine of Izumo and have the priests perform ritual prayer on their behalf.

According to the myth, the descendants of Susanoo and of Okuninushi flourished in the Izumo region, but eventually relinquished their land holdings to Amaterasu's court. Amaterasu dispatched her grandson, **Ninigi**, to rule the land, first giving him the divine mirror, which had brought her out of the cave; the divine jewel, which was hung from the *sakaki* tree in front of the cave; and the divine sword, which was discovered by Susanoo in Izumo. These "three regalia"—the mirror, the jewel, and the sword—became the symbols of the reigning emperors ever afterward. It was Ninigi's grandson, **Jinmu**, who became the first emperor (*ten'no*). This founding of the country of Japan by Jinmu is traditionally set in the year 660 B.C.E.,[13] and the imperial line carried on unbroken to the present emperor, Akihito (r. 1989–), who is the 125th emperor. In terms of the history of Japanese religions, this mytho-political account of the origin of the imperial family has additional complexities and complications, to which we shall return from time to time.

## The Ise Shrine

Every town and village in Japan has a tutelage shrine (*jinja*), but among these countless shrines, the Grand Shrine of Ise has become the "holy of holies" of Shinto shrines. For many Japanese, a pilgrimage to Ise (known as the **Ise *mairi***), at least once in their lives, is a cherished moral obligation.

The Grand Shrine of Ise was established sometime around 300 C.E., when Amaterasu, who had been enshrined in the imperial palace, was removed from the palace, because the emperor feared that he could not accord her proper worship there. He at first entrusted the care of Amaterasu to his daughter, while his aunt, Princess Yamato, went on a long journey to look for a perfect place for the goddess. Endowed with shamanic (i.e. superhuman) ability, Princess Yamato acted as a medium. When she was on the coast of **Ise**, Amaterasu instructed her: "The province of Ise, of the divine wind, is the land whither repair the waves from the eternal world, the successive waves. It is a secluded and pleasant land. In this land I wish to dwell."[14] The word "divine wind," or **_kamikaze_**, associated with the coast of Ise, henceforth became an attribute of Amaterasu, and still later symbolic of the country of Japan as divinely protected.

In the year 478, a goddess of the harvest, **Toyouke**, was moved to Ise, to keep Amaterasu company and provide her with daily food. Toyouke was given her own "Outer Shrine" (*Geku*), located a few miles away from Amaterasu's "Inner Shrine" (*Naiku*). The Ise Shrine complex also features numerous lesser deities, over one hundred in number.

*The Grand Shrine of Ise is the most sacred of all Shinto shrines. The "Inner Shrine," shown here, was established around 300 C.E. and is dedicated to the goddess Amaterasu.*

## The Institution of *Saigu* at Ise

An important feature of the Ise Shrine, dating back to the days of its founding by Princess Yamato, was the sacred office of **Saigu**. This was where the imperial princess observed rituals in honor of the goddess Amaterasu. Serving as priestesses, these princesses were called "mitsueshiro" (literally, the "august cane" on which the goddess Amaterasu relied).

The origin of *Saigu,* actually predating the shrine and its buildings, can be traced to the mandate of the early imperial court, which assumed political and religious responsibilities. The ancient theocratic origin of the Japanese political system had the emperor in charge of political affairs (**matsuri-goto**), but he was also obliged to observe (**matsuru**) proper religious rituals. Festivals (**matsuri**) were political-religious affairs. These two realms of politics and religion were gradually separated, however, and the emperor entrusted the religious observances to an unmarried daughter (or, if there was no daughter, a niece), chosen for this office by divination. The idea was that proper worship of *kami* deities was necessary in order to rule the country well. This division of responsibility—the political to the male and the religious to the female—has an ancient root (as seen with the shamanic queen Himiko, discussed above).[15]

The imperial princess who occupied the office of *Saigu* was called the **saio**, the "sacred queen." Details of the selection procedure and the itemization of her ceremonial and religious responsibilities at Ise were gradually codified and eventually set out in the *Codes of the Engi Era* (compilation begun in 905 and completed in 927). Once chosen, the princess would first spend a year in a secluded apartment in the imperial palace to undergo purification and abstinence. In the following year, she would be moved to a "palace in the field" (*nonomiya*), located in the Saga district of Kyoto, where she would undergo further purification. In the third year, she would proceed to Ise from Kyoto, taking five days, accompanied by some 200 officials, ladies-in-waiting, and other domestic helpers. In essence a "mini-court" would move with the princess from the capital to Ise. Along the way, the *saio* would stop and perform ritual purification at a number of rivers.

A princess was not normally discharged from the office of *Saigu* until her father died or abdicated. However, she was allowed to step down if her mother became seriously ill, and was forced to do so should it be discovered that she had a lover; a *saio* had to remain celibate while in office.

In 818, **Saiin**, "sacred office," a smaller replica of the office of *Saigu*, was established at the Kamigamo Shrine, in Kyoto. The imperial princess Uchiko (in office, 818–31), a beloved daughter of the emperor Saga (r. 809–23), was chosen as the first *saiin*. Both the *Saigu* and the *Saiin* systems had petered out by the end of the Kamakura period (1333), with the general decline of the imperial authority.

## *Sengu*: Periodic Rebuilding of the Shrines at Ise

A unique feature of the Ise Shrine is the custom of **sengu**—the move to new shrine buildings that takes place in both the inner and the outer compounds, every twenty years.[16] This custom poignantly illustrates how the ancient Shinto tradition is kept alive to this day, and how the lives of the people are intertwined with the activities related to the shrine.

The most recent *sengu* took place on October 2, 1993. At 8 p.m. a solemn procession walked from the older shrine building to a brand-new shrine building, in the dark, lit only by hand-held torches. All the participants were clad in Shinto priestly vestments and were led by a head priestess (probably representing the *saio*, the imperial princess who formerly acted as the head priestess of Ise). Some priests guarded the sacred object, in which the spirit of Amaterasu is believed to dwell, concealed by white curtains, while other priests carried boxes of treasures, one after another. The "move" of the deity began with a priest's cry, "Kakeko-o, kakeko-o, kakeko-o," imitating the crow of the rooster according to the myth of Amaterasu's emergence from the "Heavenly Rock Cave." The procession was accompanied by a monotonous sound of ancient flutes, which repeated the phrase C–D (do–re), an octave above middle C. Otherwise, the only thing one could hear was the sound of the feet on the gravel, as the procession made its way to the new shrine building. The actual "move" took only twenty minutes. Three days later, on October 5, 1993, the goddess of the harvest, Toyouke, was also moved from her old abode to the new shrine.

This rotation of the dwelling place of the *kami* deities originated in 690 C.E. during the reign of Empress Jito (r. 686–97). This custom has been observed fairly regularly ever since, with a few interruptions due to domestic wars, or to economic hardship within the imperial family. The next *sengu*, the sixty-second, is scheduled for the year 2013. To allow for this extensive rebuilding—there are more than 100 shrines on the Ise compound—each shrine is constructed on a lot twice the required size. Thus the new shrine can be constructed alongside the old one, which is dismantled once the new one is completed and the deity has been enshrined in it.

The periodic rebuilding of a temple may seem strange to Westerners; for in the West, religious buildings are built to last as long as possible (witness the Pantheon, the Pyramids, Chartres Cathedral, and so on). The main shrines at Ise, although built of fine wooden materials, are constructed so as to be easily dismantled. They are made of Japanese cypress (*hinoki*) trees, which are known for their tall, straight trunks and firm, smooth texture; metal is used only for ornament. The ground under the shrines is covered with white stones gathered at the nearby Miya River and transported by boat on the Isuzu River to the shrine compounds. Some three hundred thousand stones are collected for this purpose. Prior to the *sengu*, during the month of August, each pilgrim and local inhabitant is allowed to carry one stone into the sacred ground to lay it by hand. Men and women, young and old, all joyfully participate in this event.

This is the only time they can come close to the sacred sanctuary, and it is undoubtedly a special experience for them.

## The Cultural Significance of *Sengu*

Why should shrine buildings be dismantled every twenty years? This question touches the heart of the Shinto sensibility. Wooden structures, however well built, will darken in time and become less attractive. The Shinto sensibility, however, values things new and fresh, for the *kami* spirit is always new and fresh; it is ever present.By focusing on the present moment, this sensibility may account for some of Japan's achievements in such areas as technology, science, and fashion, in which being up-to-date is a paramount consideration.

Not only the shrines' buildings but also their treasures are remade for each *sengu*. Bejeweled miniature horses (horses are regarded as the suitable mode of transport for gods), ancient swords, accessories, woven fabrics, mirrors, different sorts of ceramics—all are replicated in minute detail. Thus, the techniques necessary to produce such objects must be handed down from generation to generation. Traditionally, twenty years was the time needed for a son to learn his father's skills and knowledge—another reason for the twenty-year interval between each *sengu*. In this way, the ancient techniques, artistic and otherwise, have been handed down, and the Shinto cult, culture, and industry have been sustained.

It may seem wasteful to dismantle the old shrine buildings, but most of the wood is recycled to rebuild *torii* gates (through which one enters the shrine precinct), bridges, and other smaller structures. For each *sengu*, 130,000 Japanese cypresses, more than 200 years old, are needed. Precisely because of this need for excellent trees, the art of forestry is carefully cultivated. Those entrusted with growing the Japanese cypresses needed for the future shrine buildings of Ise are a small but dedicated group. Every year, on the first workday in the shrine's forest, they offer rice wine (*sake*) to the *kami* of the mountain to pray for their safety on the job—an offering known as *oomiki*, or "sacred *sake*." After the simple ceremony the workmen themselves partake of the *oomiki*, symbolizing their participation in sacred work related to the *kami*. Because the shrine's woodsmen are dwindling in number, their wives must also contribute their time and labor to maintaining the sacred forest. This job is more than just a livelihood for these people; it gives them a higher purpose in life, which they embrace with joy and gratitude.

## Daily Activities Surrounding the Ise Shrine

The goddess Toyouke is the protector of agriculture, fisheries, and food production in general. As a thanksgiving for her work, both cooked and raw food is offered every day to the goddess, rain or shine, once in the morning and again in the afternoon. This practice has been observed since the day the Outer Shrine was established at Ise in the fifth century C.E. The utmost cleanliness is observed in the preparation of the food offering, which is cooked on a special fire, kindled each day by the priest in charge. The food-offering procession is hidden from the sight of visitors, and ends with the priest's prayers to the goddess. As part of these daily offerings local fishermen provide the bounty of the sea—including abalone, which is harvested by the female divers (*ama*) every morning. Several miles away from Ise is the small town of Futami, where the sea salt used in cooking the food offered to Toyouke is produced. Thus, the people of Ise and its vicinity have an organic kinship with the Outer Shrine, which they address as "Geku-san"—the suffix "san" expressing the personal relationship with the shrine and respect for it. Local devotees visit the shrine every morning before dawn, before beginning their daily activities.

In contrast to the Outer Shrine filled with hustle and bustle, the Inner Shrine dedicated to Amaterasu has a more formal and solemn atmosphere, befitting Amaterasu's status as the ancestor god of the imperial family. On the immaculately kept ground, majestic ancient cedar trees flank the pilgrim's path. Both at the Inner and Outer Shrines, the main buildings are shielded from view by a large white curtain-like cloth and by tall wooden hedges, leaving only the top portion of the shrine buildings visible. This half-revealed, half-concealed presence of the deity only seems to augment the mystery of the *kami*.

## The Essence of Buddhism

Buddhism, which originated in India, was transmitted to Japan via China and Korea. The founder of Buddhism, Siddhartha Gautama, was born a prince of a small tribal state under the rule of the Shakya clan.[1] At the age of 29, he renounced his throne and underwent yogic austerities, eventually to discover that religious insight could be achieved neither by extreme asceticism nor by the pursuit of pleasure but by the practice of meditation, sustained by physical well-being. This "middle way" between austerity and pleasure became a hallmark of Buddhism. Having regained his physical strength, Gautama sat under an evergreen tree and meditated on  the problem of suffering, especially as manifested in illness, old age, and death. He came to the realization that everything arises from the blind clinging to life; he further realized that if suffering arises out of a cause, then by eliminating that cause, the suffering would cease. With this realization, or "enlightenment," Gautama became the **Buddha** ("the Awakened One"). The tree under which he sat to meditate came to be known as the "bodhi" (enlightenment) tree. He opened the path of practice of insight to whoever came to him. His followers addressed him as Shakyamuni (*Shaka* in Japanese; "the sage of the Shakya clan"), Tathagata (*Nyorai* in Japanese; "Thus Come and Thus Gone One," i.e., enlightened one), or by other honorific forms of address. The Buddha taught that anyone could become a buddha by attaining insight into the cause of suffering and its cessation.

The central teaching of the Buddha has been traditionally handed down, especially in the **Theravada** tradition, in the formula of "four noble truths, eightfold path."[2] The four noble truths are as follows: (1) Life is full of suffering; (2) Suffering arises out of craving;

(3) Suffering can be stopped if craving is stopped; (4) The way to inner peace (*nirvana*) is to follow the eightfold path. The eightfold path consists of (1) right view (or wisdom); (2) right intention (or motivation); (3) right speech (in particular, honesty and kindness); (4) right conduct; (5) right means of livelihood (not harmful to others); (6) right sustained effort (to avoid evil thoughts); (7) right mindfulness; and (8) right concentration (i.e., meditation). The practice of the eightfold path promotes one's self-examination and encourages the life of spiritual-mindfulness. Although all eight elements are organically interwoven, the key is meditation, which sustains the others and brings matters into proper perspective.

During the lifetime of the Buddha, an order of monks and nuns (*sangha*) was established. Following the Buddha's death, the Buddhist community maintained its identity by upholding the "three treasures": they are the *Buddha* (the Awakened One, the ideal model for each follower), the *dharma* (teaching, universal truth, or law), and the *sangha* (religious order; also, more broadly, the community of believers).

Buddhists regard all beings as characterized by the "four marks": impermanence (nothing lasts forever); suffering (all are subjected to illness, aging, and death); no-self (there is no substance that corresponds to the "self"; the true self-identity is beyond whatever one conceives it to be); and *nirvana* (the state of equanimity attained by being liberated from the fetters of existence, or *samsara*, the cycle of life and death).

Both monastic and lay Buddhists adopt basic precepts, which are as follows: (1) Do not kill; (2) Do not steal; (3) Do not commit adultery; (4) Do not lie; and (5) Do not take intoxicants. Serious practitioners identify three "ills" that hinder their right conduct: avarice, anger, and ignorance of the Buddha's teaching. Also, conceit and jealousy are to be avoided, as they interfere with meditation. Buddhists also actively cultivate four sublime virtues: amity, or friendship; compassion; a heart that wishes for the happiness of others and rejoices with them; and equanimity.

## Hinayana and Mahayana Buddhism

Over the next few centuries, as Buddhism spread throughout India and into other Asian countries, it developed into various strands and schools, according to different interpretations of the master's teachings. The strand of Theravada Buddhism became established in Sri Lanka (Ceylon), Burma, Thailand, Laos, and Cambodia. This strand, whose name means "the path of the elders," or the learned, adheres to the original doctrine and emphasizes the strict observance of precepts, especially the monastic way of life. The second major strand was **Mahayana**—"great vehicle"—Buddhism. Its followers designated the Theravada strand as **"Hinayana,"** or "small vehicle," suggesting that the latter was relatively narrow in scope. It was mainly Mahayana Buddhism that gained a footing in Central Asia, China, Korea, and Japan, later followed by a third main strand, of **Vajrayana Buddhism**, to which we shall return later.

Mahayana Buddhism evolved as a lay movement around the first century B.C.E. Its followers asserted that their practice of Buddhism was superior to the older monastic, scholastic type of Buddhism, on the grounds that the monastic practice ultimately aimed at the attainment of spiritual enlightenment of the individual ascetic, whereas Mahayana aims to achieve the salvation of all sentient beings, which is to be carried out by the compassionate **bodhisattvas**, or "enlightenment-beings." Bodhisattvas are humans who are on their way to achieving enlightenment and yet remain in this world in order to save others; they embody the ideal of altruism.

Mahayana Buddhists developed a doctrine of the **three "bodies"** (*kaya*) or manifestations of the Buddha essence. The *nirmana-kaya* is the manifestation of the Buddha essence in the historical body of Shakyamuni Buddha; the *sambhoga-kaya* is the "reward body" enjoyed by such Buddhas as Amida (Amitabha) and **Yakushi** (Bhaisajya-guru), who attained the body of the Buddha after many eons of assiduous practice and good work as bodhisattvas; and the *dharma-kaya* is the cosmic body of Buddha, the eternal, universal Buddha-essence itself, which is manifested in nature. The *dharma-kaya* Buddha is symbolically represented by the Sun Buddha, Mahavairochana. The Mahayana pantheon is filled with various Buddhas and numerous Bodhisattvas; some of the most venerated include the Future Buddha or Miroku (Maitreya), a savior who is to appear in the human world 5 billion 670 million (5,670,000,000) years after the death of Shakyamuni, and the goddess of Mercy, Bodhisattva **Kannon**.

## The Introduction of Buddhism

Buddhism, embraced by the Chinese emperors in the first century C.E., was transmitted to Korean kingdoms in the fourth century.

The circumstances under which Buddhism was introduced to Japan were closely tied with the East Asian power politics of the fifth and sixth centuries, as Buddhism, a universal religion, was effective in forming international allies. The Korean peninsula of those days was divided into three kingdoms of Paekche, Koguryo, and Silla, each of which maintained diplomatic and military relationships with China and Japan. Japan had an interest in the Korean peninsula, because it owned a province there until 562.

In 538 King Song of Paekche (r. 523–54) sent an envoy to the Japanese emperor bearing a Buddha image cast in gold and bronze and a few Buddhist scriptures—gifts intended to secure Japan's military assistance against the invading forces of Silla. King Song's envoy also presented the emperor with a letter in which the king praised Buddhism as the "most excellent doctrine of all doctrines." Although it is "hard to explain and hard to comprehend," King Song wrote, it can "create religious merit and retribution."[3] The Japanese emperor Kinmei (r. 539–71) was delighted with this gift, but he maintained his political neutrality and did not embrace Buddhism. Instead, he gave the Buddha image to his minister, Soga no Iname. The Soga family was in charge of overseeing the revenues from wealthy Korean immigrants, whose fortunes were considerable. The Soga family cultivated close relationships with the Korean courts; they were well informed of general trends outside Japan and embraced Buddhism as the universal religion. The worship of Buddha met with staunch opposition from the Mononobe and Nakatomi families, however, who argued that if Japan were to embrace Buddhism, it would "incur the wrath of our indigenous gods."[4]

In order to conduct proper worship of the Buddha image he had been given, Soga no Iname sought out some nuns. Three daughters of distinguished families of Korean descent volunteered to take vows, and these women became the first Japanese Buddhist "monastics." Some scholars argue that the choice of women to perform this worship reflected the strong female shamanic tradition then prevalent in East Asia, including Japan.[5] Be that as it may, these nuns, together with two other women, eventually crossed the sea to Paekche, where, between 588 and 590, they studied Buddhist precepts (*Vinaya*), and were ordained. Returning to Japan, they took up their duties, while the Soga family built the first full-scale Japanese Buddhist temple for them.[6]

After many twists and turns and much opposition, the Soga family's patronage of Buddhism prevailed, and the new faith began to take root in Japan. The emperor Yomei (r. 585–87) was the first emperor to embrace both Buddhism and Shinto. Meanwhile, the Korean kingdoms continued to send to Japan accomplished Buddhist monks, nuns, temple architects, sculptors of Buddha images, and various technicians and engineers. Japanese Buddhist monks also went to Korea to study.

## Prince Shotoku

The future of Buddhism in Japan looked promising when the emperor Yomei's son, Crown Prince Shotoku (574–622), embraced the faith. Prince Shotoku is sometimes compared to the Indian king, Ashoka, who became a convert and patronized Buddhism. The prince took as his teacher the Koguryo priest, Eji (Hyeja in Korean), who was in Japan between 595 and 615; from him, Prince Shotoku attained a considerable understanding of Buddhism, including its sacred texts, or **sutras**. The prince gave an exposition of the **Queen Shrimala Sutra** (*Shoman-gyo* in Japanese) and the **Lotus Sutra** (*Hokke-kyo* in Japanese) to his aunt, Empress Suiko (r. 593–628). He also wrote a commentary on the **Vimalakirti Sutra** (*Yuima-gyo* in Japanese). (These are all Mahayana sutras.)

The *Shrimala Sutra* has as its heroine an Indian queen, whose steadfast faith in the Buddha's teachings leads her to the attainment of the highest wisdom. The spiritual mettle of the Indian queen must have appealed to the reigning empress, although she personally never embraced Buddhism, maintaining political-religious neutrality on the matter. The *Lotus Sutra* advocated the universal salvation of every single sentient being, and the *Vimalakirti Sutra* praised the lay Buddhist Vimalakirti, a wise man of considerable wealth whose understanding of Buddhism surpassed that of the wisest Bodhisattva, Manjushri (Monju in Japanese).

Prince Shotoku also studied Chinese classics with a learned Korean doctor, Kakuka (Hakka in Korean). The prince's knowledge of Confucianism, Daoism, Legalism, and other Chinese philosophical schools was considerable. He began sending envoys to the Chinese court of Sui (581–619), in order to import its culture. In 604 he issued the Seventeen-Article Constitution, which began with the celebrated line "Harmony is to be valued" and also contains the line "Sincerely reverence the three treasures."[7] Harmony is a highly esteemed Confucian virtue, while the "three treasures" constitute the heart of Buddhism—the Buddha, the teaching, and the monastic communities. Through the agency of Prince Shotoku, Buddhism, Confucianism, and other Chinese philosophical schools were incorporated into the civilization of Japan.

## The Cult of Prince Shotoku

The death of Prince Shotoku, on the fifth day of the second month of 622, plunged the entire country into deep mourning. The belief soon spread that he was a holy man; his image became merged with that of Shakyamuni Buddha, also born a prince. The account of the birth of Shotoku reads: "The Empress-consort, on the day of the dissolution of her pregnancy, went round the forbidden precinct, inspecting the different offices. When she came to the Horse Department, and had just reached the door of the stables, she was suddenly delivered of him without effort."[8] This is a clear allusion to accounts of the birth of Siddhartha (Shakyamuni), whose mother, Queen Maya, gave birth to him from her right side, without experiencing any pain; he immediately took seven steps on his own and declared to the world: "For enlightenment I was born, for the good of all that lives." Paralleling this legend of the Buddha, the praise of Shotoku's unusual ability continues: "He was able to speak as soon as he was born, and was so wise when he grew up that he could attend to the suits of ten men at once and decide them all without error. He knew beforehand what was going to happen."[9]

Thus the Shotoku cult was born. The temple closely associated with the prince, Shiten'noji, in Osaka, has become the center for his worship. Shotoku, the royal compassionate protector of Buddhism, inspired numerous Japanese Buddhists, including Saicho, Shinran, and Ippen.

## Nara Buddhism

The number of Buddhist temples in Japan increased dramatically from fewer than 80 during the Asuka period to 550 during the Hakuho period.[10] Emperors Tenmu (r. 673–86) and Monmu (r. 697–707) embraced Buddhism and laid the foundation for its patronage by the state. In 701, ecclesiastical regulations (*soni-rei*) placing the Buddhist monasteries and nunneries under government control were issued.

Imperial patronage of Buddhism continued into the Nara period, when (**Nara**) **Buddhist schools** flourished in the capital. These were Hosso (the Yogachara school), practiced in the temples of Yakushiji,

Kofukuji, and Horyuji; Kusha (the study of the *Abhidharmakosha*); Jojitsu (the study of the commentary *Satyasiddhi*); Sanron (the Madhyamika school); Kegon (the Huayan school, based on the **Flower Garland Sutra**), represented by the Todaiji temple, and Ritsu (the Vinaya or Precepts school), represented by the Toshodaiji temple. While Kusha, Jojitsu, and Ritsu were Theravada schools, Hosso and Sanron were considered early Mahayana, and Kegon fully-fledged Mahayana. Unlike the custom in the later mutually exclusive "sects," monks could freely study all the doctrines and philosophies of the different Buddhist schools to deepen their understanding of Buddhism. Moreover, at the major temples in Nara, during Buddhist festivals, music and dances were performed and simple plays were put on, which in time developed into independent arts of entertainment. Such temples as Yakushiji, Kofukuji, Horyuji, Todaiji, and Toshodaiji thrive to this day, enjoying the prestige of being the oldest temples in the country.

## The Appeal of Buddhism to the Rulers

In East Asian countries, Buddhism spread from the top down, from kings or emperors to their people. What especially appealed to the rulers was the ideal of the "wheel-turning king" (*cakravartin*), the ideal Buddhist ruler. Buddhism taught that a benevolent ruler's domain would manifest paradise on earth, and this grand concept added legitimacy to their rule. In addition, it was believed that Buddhism would protect countries ruled by pious kings.

Two Mahayana sutras, the **Golden Light Sutra** (*Konkomyo-saishoo-kyo* in Japanese) and the *Flower Garland Sutra* (*Kegon-kyo* in Japanese, *Avatamsaka Sutra* in Sanskrit), were especially important to the Japanese emperors. The *Golden Light Sutra* contains the doctrine of the Eternal Buddha and his boundless, omnipresent compassion; it also delivers the message that everyone can become a buddha by practicing selfless acts, and that religious life starts with an awareness of one's sinfulness and the desire to atone for one's sins.[11] It includes a chapter intended for kings, dealing with the right way to rule a country for the peace and happiness of all. The *Flower Garland Sutra* expounds the magnificent world of Birushana (i.e. Vairochana) Buddha, who represents the infinite Buddha essence.

## Todaiji and the Great Buddha Image

The emperor Shomu (r. 724–49) and his consort embraced Buddhism enthusiastically. The emperor ordered that copies of the *Golden Light*

*The colossal Buddha image at the Todaiji or Eastern Great Temple in Nara. Erected in 749, the image is eloquent testimony to the imperial family's passionate patronage of Buddhism.*

*Sutra* be distributed to all the provinces and that each province must erect a Buddhist monastery and a nunnery; and in 743 he ordered the erection of the head temple, Todaiji (the Eastern Great Temple), which was to serve as the center of the provincial monasteries and nunneries. He also ordered the casting of a colossal bronze Buddha image (*daibutsu*) of Vairochana Buddha. This great image, more than 50 feet (15 meters) high, was finally successfully cast in 749 after several failed attempts. Fortuitously, gold, which had been considered nonexistent in Japan, was discovered in the northern province, just in time to be used to embellish the Buddha image. For the emperor and empress (who by then had retired), gold was a gift of the compassionate Vairochana Buddha. They declared themselves to be "servants of the Three Treasures" (i.e. the Buddha, the Dharma, and the Sangha).[12] The dedication of the great Buddha statue took place in 752 in a dazzlingly glorious ceremony, performed by an Indian Buddhist monk and attended by 5,000 people.

## The Move to Kyoto

With Buddhist monasteries and nunneries being state-sponsored during the Nara period, monks and nuns were provided with their housing, robes, and food by the state. Amidst these creature comforts, some monastic Buddhists relaxed their adherence to the precepts of their faith. An extreme case was the priest of the Hosso school, Dokyo, who won the affection of the empress Shotoku (r. 764–70), and was appointed prime minister in 765. Although the empress was willing to abdicate the throne for him, she fell ill and died before that could happen, and Dokyo was banished. Finding the priests' meddling in the affairs of the state unpalatable, the emperor Kanmu (r. 781–806) moved the capital away from Nara and eventually to Kyoto.

Two great Buddhist figures emerged around this time: Saicho and Kukai. Saicho founded the Japanese Tendai sect at Mt. Hiei, and Kukai founded the Shingon sect at Mt. Koya. Both sects enjoyed the patronage of the imperial court and of aristocrats, for whose convenience they created branch temples in the city of Kyoto.

## Saicho and the Tendai Sect

Saicho (767–822), who was ordained at the Todaiji temple in 785 at the age of 19, left Nara for Mt. Hiei, where he hoped to establish more authentic Buddhist practices. His erudition and noble disposition had gained the confidence of Emperor Kanmu, and it is said that it was upon Saicho's suggestion that the emperor chose Kyoto as the site of the new capital. According to the Chinese *fengshui* practice, the northeastern corner of an area is considered the entrance of "evil spirits," and therefore it was propitious for the city to have a "fort" in that spot. Mt. Hiei is located exactly to the northeast of Kyoto, and a Buddhist monastery there was believed to protect the city from evil forces.

Saicho was convinced that the authentic practice of Buddhism could bring salvation to all sentient beings, and to that end he adopted the *Lotus Sutra* and the Chinese Tiantai treatises on meditation techniques (*shikan*) as the basic texts. With imperial backing, Saicho established a monastic center on Mt. Hiei in 794. In 804, he joined the embassy to the Chinese Tang court, bearing the mandate to receive a direct transmission of the teachings from the masters of the Tiantai (Tendai in Japanese) and the Huayan (Kegon in Japanese) schools, and to collect *sutras* and commentaries. Having fulfilled his obligation, Saicho returned to Japan the following year, bringing back 460 scrolls of *sutras* and scriptures of Buddhist schools, including meditation techniques and **esoteric Buddhist** practices (more fully introduced by Kukai, see below).

When the emperor Kanmu died in 806, Saicho lost his powerful patron, but by then the monastery on Mt. Hiei had firmly acquired a solid basis for growth and development. Every year, two students from Mt. Hiei were accepted into the fold of nationally appointed Buddhist priests. In 813, Saicho's monastic center was given the temple name of Enryakuji by the imperial court. In 818 Saicho formalized the regulations for students at Mt. Hiei; they included the number of students to be accepted at any given time, and the length of their study and training (twelve years). These regulations were made with the prospect that the place to confer Mahayana ordination would be established at Enryakuji. This privilege, Saicho's dearest wish, was granted in 822, seven days after his death. The posthumous title of Dengyo Daishi, or the "Great Master who transmitted teaching [from China]," was conferred on him in 866.

## The *Lotus Sutra* and the Guide to Tendai Meditation

The Tendai doctrine adheres to the teaching of the *Lotus Sutra*, which holds that the Buddha is eternally present, and that salvation is open to every sentient being, including even "plants and trees." The *Lotus Sutra* also spread the cult of Kannon, the bodhisattva of miraculous healing power, who delivered people from suffering, sickness, and poverty. The *Lotus Sutra* exerted a tremendous impact on the formation and development of Mahayana Buddhism. It declared itself as the supreme *sutra*,[13] and it has received the attention of leading Mahayana thinkers, starting with Nagarjuna (founder of the Indian Madhyamika school, c. 150–c. 250 C.E.). This *sutra*, translated from Sanskrit into Chinese, was accessible to the Japanese, and it will be recalled that Prince Shotoku was the first in Japan to lecture on it.

The Tendai meditation technique is known as "cessation and contemplation" (*shikan*); it involves calming the mind and deepening one's insight into the nature of the universe. The doctrine of "ichinen sanzen" (literally, "3,000 worlds [contained] in a single thought") summarizes the vast scope of Tendai meditation. It takes into account the Mahayana cosmology of "ten worlds," which are classified according to the degree of spiritual awakening of the beings belonging to each world. The ten worlds, from the lowest to the highest, are as follows: the world of those condemned to hell; of hungry ghosts; of beasts; of combative strife-ridden beings (*asuras*); of human beings; of gods; of awakened ones in the Hinayana tradition; of self-enlightened human beings; of bodhisattvas; and of buddhas. Each world is not a fixed and separate entity but is fluid, potentially containing any of the other nine worlds (for instance, in anger, a human being is more like a beast or a combative being). Thus, the ten worlds together comprise 100 "sub-worlds," as it were. Furthermore, the universe is viewed as having three dimensions: that of individuals, that of their environment (social and biological), and that of the whole cosmos. Each dimension of the universe is again characterized by the "ten worlds." Every individual (representing one of the 100 sub-worlds), belonging to any of the three dimensions of the universe in its tenfold reality (thirty aspects) simultaneously is open to 3,000 worlds. Although the actual Tendai doctrine has further layers of complexity, the purpose of meditation is to break individuals away from their self-enclosed, ego-centered perspectives, and ultimately to give rise to compassion.[14]

Saicho also incorporated the elements of esoteric rituals into Tendai practice. From the beginning, the Japanese Tendai sect was broad-based in its approach, which allowed room for various new doctrines and practices to develop. This fertile matrix produced outstanding students, some of whom would become leaders of new Buddhist movements during the Kamakura period.

## Kukai and the Shingon Sect

Kukai (774–835) was a "Renaissance man" endowed with unusual talent in such varied fields as engineering, poetry, painting, music, and languages. His Chinese is said to have been as eloquent as that of educated natives, and his calligraphic skill surpassed that of almost all his contemporaries. He was also trained in Sanskrit, the language of the original Buddhist scriptures.

Kukai's relatives groomed him for a career as a statesman, but he soon realized that his calling was religion. He favored Buddhism over Confucian and Daoist teachings, but the kind of Buddhism he was looking for was not available in Nara. Returning to Shikoku, his native island, he roamed the wilderness, subjecting himself to austere ascetic practices. He was preoccupied with the question of how the Buddha reconciled his spirituality and his natural appetites, including the sex drive. Eventually, he found the answer in the *Mahavairochana Sutra* (*Dainichi-kyo* in Japanese), in which human desires are treated positively—not as something intrinsically bad, but from the enlightened perspective, as pure.

Along with Saicho, Kukai was among the envoys sent to China in 804; there, he sought out Master Huiguo in the capital, Chang'an. Huiguo was the direct disciple of Amoghavajra, an Indian Vajrayana master, who had introduced the esoteric teachings of that practice into China. Nearing his death, Huiguo found a perfect vessel in Kukai, and he transmitted his knowledge to him in the short time that remained. Kukai returned to Japan in 806, bringing with him 247 scrolls of scriptures, mostly of the esoteric teachings, along with exquisite ***mandalas*** and all sorts of fine ritual paraphernalia.

The esoteric Buddhism that Kukai brought to Japan belongs to the third main strand of Buddhism: Vajrayana (literally, "diamond vehicle"). This form of Buddhism emerged in northern India in around the sixth or seventh century and was transmitted to Tibet, Mongolia, and China. It worships the cosmic Buddha, Mahavairochana, as the very embodiment of cosmic truth. Kukai's **Shingon** ("true word") sect developed elaborate ritual procedures, adopting the chanting of mantras and efficacious spells, and hand and finger gestures (*mudras*) to accompany each invocation. The unity of the body, the verbal expressions (recitation of *mantras*), and the intention (which focuses on the Buddha) are essential. The Shingon sect also makes extensive use of a set of paintings, called *mandalas*, which depict the doctrines expounded in the *Mahavairochana Sutra* and the *Diamond Crown Sutra* (*Kongocho-gyo* in Japanese).

In 809, three years after returning to Japan, Kukai moved to Kyoto. At that time, Saicho wished to take Kukai as his teacher and learn esoteric doctrines from him; he also sent students from Mt. Hiei to Kukai's temple for them to be trained in the esoteric practices. But when, in 815, Saicho's best student, Taihan, refused to return to Mt. Hiei and instead became Kukai's disciple, their relationship, already strained, ended. This incident led to the strict sectarianism that came to characterize the subsequent developments of Japanese Buddhism.

Kukai enjoyed the backing of Emperor Saga, who granted him land on Mt. Koya, where Kukai founded a monastery in 816 and established the Shingon sect. Kukai chose Mt. Koya because its landscape presented a natural *mandala*. The basin, on which numerous temple buildings were constructed, is surrounded by mountains, whose peaks resembled cosmic-scale lotus flower petals, each the abode of a Buddha. Kukai's teaching affirmed the importance of worldly happiness; he aimed to bring tangible and immediate benefits to people through the performance of esoteric rituals, such as the recitation of *mantras*, the burning of purifying fire, and elaborate incantation. By virtue of such aims and rituals, the Shingon sect appealed strongly to the courtiers of Kyoto, who employed priests for all kinds of occasions that demanded prayers.[15]

In 921, Kukai was given the posthumous title of Kobo Daishi, the "Great Master who spread Buddhism far and wide." Around that time a belief spread that he had not in fact died but had gone into eternal meditation in the inner sanctuary of Mt. Koya. Kukai's extraordinary charisma and spiritual gifts gave birth to the cult of "Odaishisan" (Great Teacher), which continues to be a vibrant source of inspiration for many followers. Kukai's birthday, June 15, is celebrated by a parade of lay followers from all over Japan, who gather in the mountain town of Koya and stage a colorful procession of singing and dancing. The cult of Odaishisan also gave rise to the extremely popular pilgrimage circuit on the island of Shikoku, where the young Kukai had undergone ascetic practices.

## Mountains as a Religious Training Ground

The success of Saicho and Kukai owed no small part to the locations they chose, Mt. Hiei and Mt. Koya. Both of these men were drawn to the native tradition of mountain asceticism, which went back to ancient times. To the ancient Japanese, mountains represented a kind of "border," a gateway into another world, inhabited by mysterious animals and spirits. Being sacred places, mountains were the ideal training ground for ascetics, who, by means of physical austerity, were able to hone their spiritual power to superhuman levels.[16]

One such mountain ascetic was En no Ozunu (seventh century C.E.), who is looked upon as the founder of the **Yamabushi** (mountain ascetics) cult, otherwise known as **Shugendo**. This cult combines *yin–yang* symbolism, folk religious beliefs, esoteric Buddhist cosmology, and elements of early Shinto. Followers undergo austerity in the mountains at certain times of the year. Natural geographic contours, such as caves and waterfalls, may suggest female and male features, respectively, and they were further associated with the "womb mandala" and the "diamond mandala" of the Shingon doctrine.[17]

In addition to these mountain ascetics there was a group of itinerant Buddhist ascetics (*hijiri*, "holy men") who were unaffiliated with any of the established monasteries and who traveled freely and widely to do their bodhisattva work. Among them was a monk named Gyoki, who was asked by the emperor Shomu to carry out fund-raising activities among the people in order to build the great Buddha image of Todaiji.

## The Practice of Barring Women from Sacred Mountains

When they established their mountain monasteries, both Saicho and Kukai adopted the Buddhist practice of *kekkai*—the creation of a sacred realm by the "drawing" of invisible borders, a practice that has existed since the early days of Indian Buddhism—so that students were able to concentrate on their training. The establishment of the *kekkai* meant that monastic precincts were closed to the outside world, and women, especially, were forbidden to set foot in them. The idea of *kekkai* had initially arisen from the need for rigorous spiritual training, but as the Tendai and Shingon sects became powerful institutions, the "sacred ground inaccessible to women" created a misogynist attitude on the part of the monastic community. Even nuns were forbidden from entering these monastic training grounds. At Mt. Koya, women pilgrims were obliged to stay at specifically designated buildings, called women's halls (*nyonindo*), which were placed outside the *kekkai* area. At Mt. Hiei, it appears that women were forbidden to climb the mountain after a certain demarcated point.

## Five Hindrances, Threefold Submission

The practice of barring women from mountain monastic centers seems to have given rise to the view that women were spiritually inferior to men, owing to their "**five hindrances and threefold submission**," a view that became widespread during the latter half of the Heian period. The "five hindrances" referred to the idea held by a sector of Indian Buddhists that a woman could not become any of the Hindu deities—Brahma (the godhead), Indra (the god of fire), or Papiyas (the god who enjoys all desires)—nor a sage-king, nor an enlightened sage.[18] Coupled with this was the traditional view of women, which was widely held in Asia, that women were subjected to the "threefold submission"—namely, a woman in her childhood has to obey her father; when married, obey her husband; and in old age, obey her son. The idea of "five hindrances, threefold submission" (*gosho sansho* in Japanese) cast a shadow of doubt over women's spiritual prowess, despite the Buddhist message of universal salvation.

A poet of the Heian period, Lady Izumi Shikibu (c. 978–sometime after 1036), wistfully describes in one of her poems her feelings on seeing one of the Mt. Hiei monks walking back to his abode while carrying a wildflower, an *ominaeshi*, in his hand. Written in Chinese character, the word "ominaeshi" is made up of the characters, "woman," "folk," and "flower," and for Lady Izumi, the flower is a representation of sisterhood.

> If you are true to your name,
> You should be burdened with
> "Five hindrances."
> How I envy you!
> You, flower, ascending the hill.[19]

## Folk Beliefs and Popular Religious Practices

Despite the success of Buddhism in Japan it did not take over nor overshadow the rich diversity of folk religious practices. In fact, if anything, Buddhist elements added further complexity to popular religious beliefs. These religious practices are still part of Japanese life.

Many popular beliefs bear the influence of **onmyodo** (literally, the *yin–yang* practice), which comprises astrology, fortune-telling, *fengshui* practice, and numerous calendrical taboos. These were introduced into Japan from China via Korea, along with Buddhism, Confucianism, and religious Daoism. During the reign of Emperor Tenmu, the office of calendar (or Onmyo-ryo) was established, where learned doctors engaged in advising people on auspicious and inauspicious days and the time of the day for certain activities, as well as directions to be avoided. (One only needs to read a section of *The Tale of Genji*, written c. 1000 C.E., to see how these taboos hampered the lives of the people.) Since then, many old fears and taboos have died out, but new calendrical jinxes have been added (something similar to the sentiment of "Friday the thirteenth"). Today, the six-day calendrical cycle of auspicious, semi-auspicious, and inauspicious days, widely adopted during the Edo period, still influences the activities of the Japanese people when it comes to scheduling important events, such as a wedding or a funeral, or opening a new business.

Almost all Shinto shrines and some Buddhist temples sell omikuji or "fortune-telling slips," which generally divine one's current state in terms of luck (something similar to the Western horoscope). These slips typically contain a didactic poem, on which one is supposed to reflect in order to better one's luck. These days, popular temples and shrines carry omikuji in English, too.

## Fear of Retribution by Angry Spirits

During the Heian period, a belief spread that the spirits of court nobles who had died in exile as victims of political intrigues haunted the living and brought about calamities and diseases. It was also believed that proper worship could pacify a *goryo* (the vengeful spirit of the wronged) or **onryo** (angry spirit). In the mid-ninth century the Yasaka Shrine was erected in Kyoto to pacify one of the angry spirits, now deified. When a plague broke out in Kyoto in 876, it exacerbated this fear among the city's inhabitants—of all social backgrounds—and a festival was organized to pacify the angry spirits. This was the beginning of Kyoto's famous Gion Festival.

One of the most popular types of shrine in modern-day Japan, especially among students and their parents, is the Tenmangu shrine, which can be found throughout the country. The shrine's origin goes back to the cult of Sugawara no Michizane (845–903). Michizane, a deputy prime minister, became the victim of a court intrigue and in 901 was exiled to Dazaifu on Kyushu, where he died brokenhearted. In the year 930, a devastating thunderstorm struck the private apartments of the imperial palace, killing several ministers and causing the emperor to become fatally ill. The rumor spread that this was the doing of the ghost of Michizane. Prior to these thunderstorms there had already been numerous signs of Michizane's anguish, and in 923 his former title of deputy prime minister had been restored and the highest court rank posthumously bestowed on him. But it was clear to the frightened courtiers that more had to be done to pacify Michizane's spirit. In 947 a Tenmangu shrine was erected to house his spirit, and he was apotheosized as a *kami*, Tenjin. Since Michizane had been a man of extraordinary erudition, he became the patron of learning and scholarship. Today, school children and students will flock to a Tenmangu shrine; each purchases a charm (*omamori*), dedicates a votive wooden tablet (*ema*), and has the shrine priest pray for good grades and success in school entrance examinations. These are but a few examples of the many ancient religious practices that survive in modern Japan.

# The Rise of Kamakura Buddhist Sects

## The Amida Cult and *Nenbutsu*

Traditionally, Buddhists have shared the view—formulated in China—that, in time, the Buddha's teaching would gradually decline. In Japan the final "period of the end of teaching" (**mappo**) was expected to commence in the year 1052.[1] As this time approached, people were beset by uncertainty and anxiety. They turned to Buddhas and Bodhisattvas for their salvation, especially to Amida Buddha.

Amida Buddha is the hero of the **Greater Pure Land Sutra** (*Daimuryoju-kyo* in Japanese). According to this *sutra*, when he was a bodhisattva, Dharmakara, he took forty-eight vows to save all sentient beings. His eighteenth vow declared that he would not become a Buddha if anyone invoked his help at their moment of death and he failed to stand before them with the "community of mendicants." After eons of assiduous bodhisattva practice, Dharmakara fulfilled his vows and became a Buddha, Amitabha (Amida in Japanese). Thus, anyone who invokes his name for help is reborn in Amida's Western Paradise.

### Genshin and the Pictures of Paradise and Hell

It is said that the practice of **nenbutsu**—the continuous invocation of Buddha Amida's name, "Namu Amida-butsu"—was first brought to Japan from China in 847 by a Tendai priest named En'nin. The practice gradually spread among the monks of Mt. Hiei and gained momentum. In 964 those who devoted themselves solely to the practice of *nenbutsu* formed a society under the guidance of Genshin (942–1017).

Genshin was largely responsible for the spread of the Amida cult beyond the community of monks at Mt. Hiei. In his *Essentials of*

*Amida Buddha, atop auspicious clouds and surrounded by bodhi-sattvas, comes down to earth to receive the faithful to his Pure Land. Paintings on this theme, known as* raigo, *were popular during the medieval period.*

*Salvation*, he depicted "ten realms of existence" or "ten worlds" (see Chapter 3), extending from the world of hell to the world of buddhas or paradise. Genshin stressed the idea that one's deeds in this world determine the world into which one will be reborn in the next life. Especially powerful was Genshin's graphic depiction of eight hells (the hell of the pool of blood, the hell of fire, and so forth): they were so ghastly that people wished to avoid hell at all costs and be reborn in paradise. Genshin, a gifted artist, expressed his vision in paintings and sculptures. Paintings on the theme of *raigo*— Amida Buddha coming down on a golden cloud from his Western

Paradise accompanied by a host of benevolent bodhisattvas to rescue a faithful person on his deathbed—made a strong impression.

In this religiously-charged period, even the most powerful approached death with careful preparation to increase their chances of rebirth in paradise. In 1027, the prime minister Fujiwara no Michinaga breathed his last while holding onto five colored strings (blue, yellow, red, white, and black), which were tied to the hand of an image of Amida Buddha. Such a manner of dying was believed to ensure one's rebirth in the Western Paradise. In the critical year of 1052, Michinaga's son, Yorimichi, also a prime minister, converted his magnificent villa in Uji, south of Kyoto, into the Buddhist temple of Byodoin, and the following year he had enshrined a large gilded image of Amida Buddha in its main hall.

## The Rise of "Kamakura Buddhism"

During the Kamakura period, great religious leaders emerged one after another. Such sects as the Pure Land (**Jodo-shu**), the True Pure Land (**Jodo Shin-shu**), the **Rinzai** and the **Soto Zen**, the **Nichiren**, and the Timely (**Ji-shu**)—all destined to become major Japanese Buddhist sects—arose during this time. They are sometimes collectively called Kamakura Buddhism. These sects brought the message of Buddhist salvation into the city streets and remote hamlets. Moreover, the leaders of these new Buddhist movements flatly rejected the idea of the inferiority of women's spirituality. They welcomed women into their congregations, guaranteeing every woman an equal chance of religious salvation and encouraging women to practice Buddhism.[2] Their active proselytizing of women contributed to the phenomenal evangelical success of these new sects.

### Honen and the Pure Land Sect

Honen (1133–1212) founded the Pure Land sect (Jodo-shu in Japanese). He had been a promising scholar-monk at Mt. Hiei, but abandoned its elite path in his dedication to the mission of Buddhism—the salvation of every person. His mentor at Mt. Hiei, impressed by his prowess, gave him the Buddhist name of Honen, "Dharma-just-so." After eighteen years of intensive study of Buddhist scriptures, he came upon a commentary on the *Sutra on the Visualization of the Pure Land* (*Kanmuryoju-kyo* in Japanese) by a Chinese Pure Land master,

Shandao (Zendo in Japanese). Shandao held that everyone is saved by steadfast practice of *nenbutsu*, as is promised by Amida Buddha. For Honen, this was the scriptural basis to support his conviction that single-minded, sustained recitation of *nenbutsu* was the gateway to Amida's Paradise.

Honen then sat down to systematize his thought by selectively choosing and discarding passages from the Mahayana scriptures. He divided Buddhist practice into the "path of the Pure Land" and the "path of personal sanctity." The former relied on the absolute compassion of Amida (i.e. the other-power or **tariki**) and was, therefore, the "easy path." The latter was the path of personal effort (self-power or **jiriki**) and, therefore, a "difficult path"; this he discarded. Next, he divided the "path of the Pure Land" into "essential" practice, which would lead one to attain rebirth in Amida's Paradise, and "nonessential" practices, discarding the latter. Next, he divided the path of "essential practice" into "main activity" (i.e. the recitation of *nenbutsu*) and "auxiliary activities" (such as the recitation of the Pure Land *sutras* and the ritual worship of Amida), and deemed the former to be the more important.[3] Thus, Honen established his doctrine that the practice of sincere, uninterrupted, sustained recitation of *nenbutsu* was all that was necessary for one to attain salvation.

Honen's conviction of the power of *nenbutsu* was confirmed when he encountered a monk, Ensho, who was known for his passionate practice of continuous *nenbutsu* and radiated sanctity and gratitude, which came from a life dedicated to *nenbutsu*. It should be noted that prior to Honen there were already precursors of *nenbutsu* practice: Kuya (903–972), an itinerant monk, spread the *nenbutsu* practice among the people and was revered as the "saint of the streets"; and Ryonin (1072–1132), an accomplished priest trained at Mt. Hiei, founded the sect of Yuzu-nenbutsu in 1117 with imperial permission.

Honen began his missionary activities, advocating the constant recitation of *nenbutsu*, or *senju nenbutsu*. Along with his evangelical activities, he trained disciples, who numbered 190, each of whom had about 200 followers, and thus founded his own religious order. Honen took an egalitarian stance with regard to women, whom he regarded as equally deserving of Amida's Paradise; and his nobility of soul attracted a wide range of female followers, from imperial princesses to the lowliest "women of pleasure."

With the growing popularity of Honen's teachings, *nenbutsu* practitioners became a force to be reckoned with. Perceiving a potential threat, the monasteries of Enryakuji (the center of Tendai Buddhism) and Kofukuji (the center of the Hosso school in Nara) filed a petition with the imperial court in 1204 and 1205 respectively, requesting a ban on the practice of *nenbutsu*. The imperial court issued an order in 1207 which condemned to death two of Honen's direct disciples who had powerful political connections, and exiled Honen and his main disciples. An imperial pardon allowed Honen to return to Kyoto in November 1211; but exhaustion and the hardship he had suffered during his exile hastened his death. He died two months later, at the age of 80.

An anecdote has it that as Honen neared death, his disciples began to prepare five colored strings and a scroll of painting, depicting Amida coming to receive the faithful. Noticing this activity, Honen said: "I originally came from Amida's paradise, and I'm now returning to it. Don't bother with anything."[4] In his last days, Honen wrote down his lifelong convictions in his *One-Page Testament*, which reads, in part: "The method of final salvation . . . is nothing but the mere recitation of the 'Namu Amida-butsu,' without any doubt of His mercy, and whereby one may be born into the Land of Perfect Bliss."[5]

The Jodo sect thrives to this day, and has some 6,500,000 followers. It has also established universities which train Buddhist priests and scholars.

## Shinran and the True Pure Land Sect

One of Honen's disciples, named Shinran (1173–1262), was the founder of the True Pure Land sect (Jodo Shin-shu in Japanese). Shinran, too, was trained at Mt. Hiei, but while there he was tormented by his sexual desires. During the day, he was able to control his urges, but in sleep he would dream of making love to women. His sense of guilt over this deepened his consciousness of sinfulness. To relieve his agony, Kannon, bodhisattva of mercy, appeared in a dream and told him: "I will become your wife and alleviate your sufferings." Shinran then left Mt. Hiei and joined Honen's order in 1201. In Honen's view, having a wife need not hinder one's religious practice or diminish one's chances of salvation. Thus encouraged, Shinran got married but still remained a man of religion, and began a lifestyle of being "neither a monk nor a layman."

Shinran was among those exiled in 1207, along with Honen and other disciples. In exile, Shinran lived among ordinary people, who began to form a strongly knit religious community around him. It was only when he was about 60 years old that he returned to Kyoto. There, he poured his energy into completing his major work, *Kyogyoshinsho* (*Doctrine, Practice, Faith, and Testimony*). Shinran also wrote many other religious works, including hymns. He died in 1262 at the age of 89.

The *Tan'nisho*, a compilation of Shinran's sayings and confessions, reveals Shinran the confessor. He held that "if even good people are reborn in the Pure Land, how much more so are the wicked!" His reasoning was that repentant sinners throw themselves entirely on the mercy of Amida, while the good might think that their good conduct would improve their chances of salvation.[6] It is harder for the good to get rid of their implicit self-confidence, whereas a sinner knows that he is as helpless as a baby. It was Shinran's utter abandonment of reliance on "self-power" that distinguished him from his master. Honen held that continuous selfless invocation of Amida's name was the path to salvation, but Shinran came to believe that a "single sincere invocation is enough"; for him, continuous invocation still held a residue of self-reliance. Radically simplifying Honan's teaching, Shinran declared that devotion to Amida Buddha was enough and that Shakyamuni Buddha was merely an instrument for reaching Amida. He also held that the only *sutra* essential to salvation was the *Greater Pure Land Sutra* (*Daimuryoju-kyo*). He forbade his followers to worship the *kami* and to observe widespread popular calendrical taboos, condemning them as superstitions.

Shinran's followers formed the independent sect of Jodo Shinshu, also known as the Ikko sect—*ikko* meaning "single-minded and steadfast." Because its priests were allowed to marry, the leadership became hereditary. Today, its head temples are Nishi Honganji and Higashi Honganji, both in Kyoto; and the sect, which is the largest Buddhist sect in Japan, has a following of some 13,000,000—about 25 percent of the entire Japanese Buddhist population.

## Zen or the Meditation School

While the Pure Land tradition emphasizes faith in the saving grace of Amida and the practice of *nenbutsu* chanting, the various Zen schools emphasize the individual's personal effort to achieve spiritual awakening (*satori*), emulating Shakyamuni Buddha's practice of sitting meditation. In fact, the Japanese word "**Zen**," derived from the Chinese "**Chan**," is a phonetic approximation of the Sanskrit word *dhyāna*, "concentration meditation."

The meditation school was introduced into China by an Indian monk, Bodhidharma, around the year 520, and various lineages of Chan Buddhism developed in China, many of which were transmitted to Japan. The three major Japanese Zen sects are Rinzai, Soto, and **Obaku** (see Chapter 6), which are further divided into a number of different lineages. Today, those who support Zen temples (all sects combined) account for about 10 percent of the Japanese Buddhist population.

Common to all branches of Zen Buddhism is the practice of sitting meditation, or **zazen**. The practitioner sits up straight in the "lotus position," with legs crossed, the palm of the left hand placed on the palm of the right hand with thumbs lightly touching each other, the eyes looking down on the floor and focused at a point about a yard (one meter) ahead, and the mind concentrating on breathing in and out. Because of the unison of physical and mental concentration, Zen adepts speak of zazen as mind–body practice.

The initial goal of the practitioner is to attain "breakthrough" (kensho), which is the entrance to the attainment of "enlightenment" (satori). The satori experience may or may not take place at one single moment; for some individuals, it may come as a gradual dawning experience. Zen masters do not consider the experience of breakthrough (kensho) or the attainment of satori as the ultimate goal of Zen practice but rather the entering point to the real practice. Also, some masters maintain that lifelong practice is itself enlightenment— a teaching especially characteristic of the Soto sect. The Rinzai sect, in contrast, adheres to quickening the process of breakthrough, kensho, by adopting a **koan** (originally, a legal case before court), a problem for students to meditate and solve. Students "sit on" the koan given by the master, until the answer emerges, or until the koan dissolves of itself and no longer presents a "case" to be pondered. The koan practice challenges the epistemological dichotomy of subject and object, the mind and the body. A koan is not a "question" in the ordinary sense of the word, but a device to help the student break away from the habit of objective thinking and restore the original subject–object unity. "Does a dog have the buddha nature?" or "What is the sound of one hand clapping?" are typical koan that might be given to a novice. Once established in the mental posture acquired through the zazen practice, Zen adepts maintain this mental posture in whatever they do, whether it be sports, cooking, walking, reading, or scholarly pursuits.

The basic stance of Zen came to be formulated in four lines:

*Kyoge betsuden*
*Furyu monji*
*Jikishi nin'shin*
*Kensho jobutsu*

"The real teaching is transmitted independent of any Buddhist scriptures; it is transmitted not by way of words [but from heart to heart since the time of the Buddha]; it directly points to the human heart [which is none other than the buddha nature]; and by realizing one's true self, one attains buddhahood."

## Eisai and the Rinzai Zen Sect

The Rinzai lineage of Zen was introduced to Japan from China in 1191 by Eisai (or more properly, Yosai, 1141–1215). Eisai received his ordination at Mt. Hiei at the age of 14. His lifelong wish was to make a pilgrimage to India, the birthplace of Buddhism, but India was too far away, and he had to settle for China (a country with which Japan was engaging in frequent trade). He made two trips to Song China, in 1158 and 1187. His second sojourn lasted for four years, during which time he practiced under Master Xuan Huaichang (Kian Esho in Japanese) at the Tiantong monastery. After returning to Japan in 1191 Eisai founded two Zen temples in northern Kyushu—Hoonji and Shofukuji. In addition to Zen Buddhism, Eisai also brought with him some seeds of the tea plant; he praised tea as "the most wonderful medicine for nourishing one's health; it is the secret of long life."[7]

Eisai wanted to build a Zen temple in Kyoto, but the Mt. Hiei monastery fiercely opposed it. Wishing the emperor's court to understand what Zen teaching was all about, Eisai wrote a treatise, *Propagation of Zen for the Protection of the Country* (*Kozen gokokuron*), in 1198. Zen, he argued, investigates the true nature of consciousness (that is, mind), which is limitless and contains everything on earth and in the universe. Consciousness is the real manifestation of the universe itself. Zen also teaches how to "kill" one's ego. Unless one becomes pure and simple, one cannot embody the universal truth. Therefore, to promote Zen is to promote unselfishness; this, Eisai held, would lead to the protection of the country and the creation of a peaceful society.[8]

In 1199 Eisai traveled to Kamakura, the seat of the new shogunate, where he gained the patronage of Hojo Masako, the widow of shogun Minamoto Yoritomo, and established a Zen temple, Jufukuji. Because the objection of the Mt. Hiei monastery was still strong and Zen was not yet welcome, Eisai opened this temple under the lineage of Tendai Buddhism, but he carefully promoted Zen practice among his close disciples.

Gradually, Eisai's effort to transplant Zen onto Japanese soil began to bear fruit. In 1202, the shogunate granted him permission to build a Zen temple in Kyoto. It was to this temple, Ken'ninji, that the young Dogen came to practice Zen under Eisai. Dogen fondly remembered Master Eisai and gave testimony to him in his *Primer of Soto Zen* (*Shobogenzo zuimonki*).[9]

## Dogen and the Soto Zen Sect

Dogen (1200–53) was born into the family of an eminent courtier. At the age of 13 he was ordained at Mt. Hiei by the head priest of the Tendai sect, but the following year he left Mt. Hiei to become Eisai's disciple at Ken'ninji. On Eisai's death a year later, Dogen continued his studies with Eisai's successor, Myozen. In 1223, Dogen and Myozen crossed the sea to Song China; there, in 1225, Dogen took Rujing (Nyojyo in Japanese), new abbot of the Tiantong monastery, as his teacher. Myozen, by then very ill, died. Rujing and Dogen struck an instant teacher–disciple bond, and under his new master's guidance, Dogen attained enlightenment.

Dogen returned to Japan in 1228, bringing back Myozen's ashes with him. In 1233 he established the Koshoji temple in Uji. Since Rujing belonged to the Caodong (Soto in Japanese) lineage, Dogen brought this Chan tradition back to his homeland, even though he had not intended to found a separate school of Zen. Over the next ten years he trained his disciples—who included nuns and female lay followers—while he wrote his *General Advice on the Principles of Zazen* (*Fukan zazen-gi*). He also began writing sermons and advice for his disciples; these eventually became the monumental *Eye Treasures of the Right Dharma* (*Shobogenzo*). In 1243 Dogen was invited to Echizen, deep in the mountains, where he established a monastery, Eiheiji ("temple of eternal peace"). Dogen's health began to decline in 1253, and he moved back to Kyoto, where he died at the age of 53.

The young Dogen had one question: If we are already enlightened, as the Tendai doctrine claims, what is the meaning of Buddhist practice, and why is it necessary? The answer to his question was "Just sit, and sit through" (*shikan taza*). One does not sit *in order to* attain enlightenment. *Zazen* practice has no utilitarian goal; it is, rather, the end in itself. For this reason, Dogen did not find the use of a *koan* particularly necessary; more important for him was the practice of "just sitting." In and through sitting one comes to see face to face one's original buddha nature and enters the realm of freedom. For Dogen, the monastic life was the noblest of callings.

Very close to Dogen's heart was the image of Gautama Buddha sitting under the bodhi tree in deep meditation. For Dogen, the practice of sitting meditation was the direct link to original Buddhism. In this spirit, he preferred to call his teachings "Buppo" (Buddha's teachings) rather than "Zen." A purist, who wished to have no tie with secular political authorities, he refused the invitation by the shogunate to establish a Zen temple in Kamakura.

## Patronage of Zen by the Kamakura Shogunate

The Hojo regents in Kamakura patronized Zen, as it brought with it vibrant Chinese culture, which seemed to elevate the cultural status of the shogunate in relation to the imperial court in Kyoto.[10] Hojo Tokiyori (r. 1246–54), the only regent to personally embrace Zen practice, trained under a Chinese master, Gottan Funen (1197–1276). He extended his sponsorship to another Zen master from China, Rankei Doryu (1213–78), who moved to Japan in 1246 and in 1253 founded Kenchoji monastery, in Kamakura. He laid out the monastery following the tradition prevalent during the Song dynasty. Rankei's reputation was such that 700 monks enrolled in Kenchoji to train. Rankei's disciple, Nanpo Shomyo, or Daio (1235–1308), trained Shuho Myocho, also known as Daito (1282–1337), the founder of Daitokuji temple in Kyoto.[11] The retired emperor Hanazono and the emperor Godaigo both took Daito as their spiritual teacher. Daio and Daito trained Kanzan Egen (1277–1360), who established the Myoshinji temple in Kyoto. This lineage of Rankei–Daio–Daito–Kanzan came to represent one of the most influential lineages of Japanese Rinzai Zen.

Following Tokiyori's example the Hojo regents generally supported Zen Buddhism, and toward the end of the thirteenth century several accomplished Chinese masters emigrated to Japan at the regent's invitation. Mugaku Sogen (1226–86) arrived in Japan in 1279 and succeeded Rankei to the abbacy of Kenchoji. In 1282, Mugaku founded Engakuji in Kamakura; he also trained Koho Ken'nichi (1241–1316), a son of the emperor Gosaga. The development of the Rinzai Zen sect thus owed much to the Chinese Chan masters who settled in Japan.

## Laying the Foundations for the Five Mountain Culture

The Chinese cultural components that Zen Buddhism introduced to the Japanese were attractive to the Hojo regents, who were eager to attain cultural sophistication. Regent Hojo Sadatoki (r. 1284–1303) designated five Zen temples in Kamakura and five in Kyoto as cultural centers, and gave them special patronage. Various forms of literature, including the composition of poetry in Chinese, as well as calligraphy and ink painting, flourished at these temples. During the Muromachi period that followed, these Zen temples became the centers of the "**five mountain** [i.e. five temple] **culture**." Many eminent Chinese masters, notably Issan Ichinei (1247–1317), laid the foundations for the development of Japanese monastic Zen culture. Issan was well-versed in Neo-Confucianism, as well as in Chinese literature and classics, and was a gifted calligrapher and connoisseur of Chinese painting. The emperor Gouda (r. 1303–08) appointed him to the abbacy of Nanzenji, in Kyoto, and practiced Zen under him.

## Nichiren and the Lotus Sect

Like other religious leaders of the Kamakura period, Nichiren (1222–82) was trained at Mt. Hiei, where he cultivated profound respect for Saicho, and developed his conviction that the teaching of the *Lotus Sutra* alone contained the real teachings of Shakyamuni Buddha. In 1253, having completed his twelve years of training, he moved to Kamakura, close to his native village. Around this time, he changed his name to Nichiren—written with two Chinese characters, "sun" and "lotus"—which encapsulated his ardent devotion to Japan (which in Chinese characters is written as "sun-source") and his great esteem of the *Lotus Sutra*. Nichiren was a charismatic preacher and soon began to attract many followers, especially from among the class of wealthy landowners and their wives.

In 1257, a terrible earthquake flattened Kamakura. Torrential rains, floods, thunderstorms, mountain fires, and other calamities followed each other in close succession, greatly afflicting the lives of the inhabitants. Many people died of starvation or as a result of outbreaks of smallpox. Earlier, in the political arena, the imperial court had in 1221 launched a rebellion against the shogunate; the rebellion had been crushed and the emperor deposed. Nichiren took these occurrences as signs of deeper trouble and concluded that the decline in social mores and the endless natural calamities were the result of the withering away of the bodhisattva practice of perseverance and self-sacrifice, as expounded in the *Lotus Sutra*. He attributed the social and political problems especially to the prevalence of the Pure Land *nenbutsu* practice.

In 1260 Nichiren wrote the *Establishment of the Legitimate Teaching for the Security of the Country (Rissho ankoku-ron)*; he presented it to the regent and urged him to suppress the practice of the Pure Land sect. He also warned that unless the country were ruled according to the teachings of the *Lotus Sutra*, there would be internal political upheavals and foreign invasions. His pointed attack on Pure Land sects incited anger among some shogunate officials, who had him exiled to Ito, on the Izu peninsula, where he remained for two years.

In 1268 the Mongols sent an envoy to Japan, demanding tribute. This incident convinced Nichiren that his prediction of foreign invasion was becoming a reality. Emboldened, he wrote letters to the Japanese authorities, reminding them of his warnings. In his letter to the Rinzai Zen master Rankei Doryu, Nichiren insulted other religious sects (with the exception of the Tendai) thus: "*Nenbutsu* practice leads the country to infinite hell; Zen is the deeds of the tempter-devils; Shingon promotes the evil law that ruins the country; *Vinaya* [the old Nara schools] are the liars, the nation's bandits." This furious accusation again resulted in Nichiren's exile in 1271, this time to the northern island of Sado. Nichiren became convinced that he was a martyr and reasoned that whatever hardship he had to suffer was the price of his misconduct in former lives. While in exile on Sado, he composed his testament, *Opening the Eyes (Kaimokusho)*, in which he spelled out his mission, which was to "uphold the *Lotus Sutra*," and to become "the pillar of Japan, the eye of Japan, and the great ship [to save the people] of Japan." Nichiren thus founded the *Hokke* or Lotus sect, which is also known as the *Nichiren* sect. In the place of *nenbutsu* practice, he adopted the recitation of "Homage to the Marvelous Teachings of the *Lotus Sutra*" or "Namu Myoho-rengekyo."

In 1274 Nichiren was pardoned, and he returned to Kamakura in March. Realizing that his warnings went unheeded by the shogunate, he retreated to a hermitage on Mt. Minobu in May. In October of that year, a 25,000-strong Mongol army invaded Kyushu, but was destroyed by a typhoon. A second Mongol invasion came in 1281, and this, too, was destroyed by a typhoon. By then, Nichiren was in frail condition; he died on October 13, 1282, surrounded by his devoted followers and disciples.

## Ippen and the Ji Sect

Yet another Buddhist evangelist, Ippen (1239–89), was born into a wealthy family which had amassed its riches by piracy. At the age of 13 he became a novice and began training under the Pure Land master Shodatsu, in Kyushu. When his father died, Ippen, now 25, was compelled to return to secular life and assume family responsibilities. He got married and led the life of a householder. Eventually, however, his religious urge got the better of him. In 1271 he made a pilgrimage to Zenkoji, a popular pilgrimage destination for the devotees of the Pure Land faith; two years later, he went on a pilgrimage to Mt. Kumano.

While in Kumano, Ippen received in a dream an oracle from Kumano **Gongen**, a *kami* deity and avatar of the Buddha essence, directing him to begin his evangelical activities. He renounced his family and family fortune, and became an itinerant preacher, traveling on foot throughout the country. Wherever he went, he gave out "the proof of salvation" to whoever came to him. This was a piece of paper on which Ippen had written, in Chinese characters: "Namu Amida-butsu, Six Hundred Thousand People will Definitely be Reborn [into the Amida's Paradise]."

In a short time Ippen had acquired a number of disciples and began to achieve mass conversions. His ever-increasing followers formed a sect, called the "Timely" sect, or *Ji-shu*. Ippen introduced song and dance to the *nenbutsu* practice, and this "dancing *nenbutsu*" became the signature of the Ji sect's practice. Ippen never settled in one place for long until the very end of his life. He died on August 23, 1289, at the age of 51.

What drove Ippen was his acute sense of the transience of life and his wish to help ease people's fear of dying. He took Kuya, the tenth-century itinerant *nenbutsu* practitioner, as one of his models. But his primary model was Shakyamuni Buddha, who renounced everything and lived the life of an itinerant preacher. For Ippen, "renunciation" went far deeper than a renunciation of material goods; ultimately it was the renunciation of one's hubris and ego-centered perspective on life.[12]

Because Ippen was not interested in establishing an organized sect or a monastery, the Ji sect lacked the institutional basis to grow into a powerful force. Nonetheless, the sect survives to this day, with its head temple of Shojokoji located in Fujisawa, in Kanagawa Prefecture.

## Shinto–Buddhism Interaction and Fusion

The relationship between Shinto and Buddhism has sometimes been cordial and other times antagonistic. From the mid-Heian period onward, however, these two traditions were to a large degree amalgamated—a phenomenon known as **shinbutsu shugo** (literally,  "overlapping of Shinto and Buddhism"). No doubt this was in large part due to the fact that by this time the Tendai and Shingon sects were firmly established, and had extended their reach to incorporate Shinto deities within their institutions.

The introduction of Buddhism into Japan was initially met with resistance, as we have seen, from those who adhered to Shinto; but Buddhism soon began to put down roots. During the Nara period, Shinto *kami* deities were considered to protect the Buddhist doctrines (*dharma*). For instance, the Shinto *kami* Hachiman, of the Usa Shrine in Kyushu, was given the title of "Bodhisattva" (*Bosatsu*) in 746 for the support it had rendered to the successful completion of the construction of the great Buddhist temple of Todaiji, in Nara. Around this time, the *kami* worshipped by local powerful clans were woven into a Buddhist framework.

According to the Indian Buddhist tradition, native Indian gods (*devas*) were considered not fully enlightened and were therefore subject to the law of karmic bondage, *samsara*. Residing in the world just one rung above human beings, the *devas* could fall down from heaven—in contrast to the perfectly enlightened sages and Buddhas, who enjoyed eternal bliss. Accordingly, a belief spread in Japan that the Shinto *kami* could improve their lot by taking refuge in Buddhism. "Shrine-temples," or **jinguji**, were erected on the precincts of Shinto shrines, so that the *kami* could undergo Buddhist practice and attain bud-dhahood. Extensive "conversion" of Shinto deities to Buddhism took place from the Nara to the early Heian period.

Both Saicho, the founder of the Tendai sect, and Kukai, the founder of the Shingon sect, accorded profound respect to the native *kami* spirits. Saicho took the ancient deity Ooyamagui as the protector god of Mt. Hiei and made the Hie Shrine (known as Hiyoshi Taisha today) in Sakamoto, on the eastern foothills of Mt. Hiei, the seat of this deity. (Mt. Hiei was in fact named after the Hie Shrine.) Likewise, Kukai enshrined the goddess Niutsu, her son Kariba, and more than 100 *kami* deities from around Mt. Koya as the protector deities of that mountain. Legend has it that the **myojin** Kariba, the spirit of Mt. Koya, offered his two companion dogs, "Shiro" ("White") and "Kuro" ("Black") to assist Kukai in finding the preordained site where he was to con-struct his monastery. In order to venerate these *kami*, Kukai built a special shrine, *Miyashiro*, in the heart of the monastic compound at Mt. Koya.

## The "Essence-Manifestation" Theory

Another approach to reconciling Shinto and Buddhism was the theory of "**essence-manifestation**," or *honji-suijaku*, which became popular in the tenth century in Japan.[1] According to this theory, the *kami* were considered manifestations of the Buddha essence. For example, the *kami* of the sacred mountain Kumano came to be called "Gongen," meaning the "provisional manifestation of the Buddha essence in the guise of *kami*." (It was this Kumano Gongen, inci-dentally, that appeared in Ippen's dream [see Chapter 4] and delivered the oracle.) Gradually, one-to-one correspondence between a *kami* and a particular Buddha or Bodhisattva was drawn up. The sun goddess Amaterasu was identified as the manifestation of the sun Bud-dha, Mahavairochana; the god Hachiman was the manifestation of Amida Buddha; the goddess of the Itsukushima Shrine (which was the tutelage shrine of the Taira, or Heike, clan) was the manifestation of Kannon, and so forth.[2] Every *kami* now had a corresponding Buddhist "origin." Under the influence of Buddhism, images of *kami*, fashioned after those of Buddhas and Bodhisattvas, were created and venerated at Shinto shrines.

The most salient case of the hybrid nature of Buddhism and Shinto was Ryobu Shinto. With ryobu meaning "twofold," "double," or "dual," the idea was derived from the Shingon view of the worlds in terms of the womb mandala and the diamond mandala. Ryobu Shinto identified Mahavairochana of the Shingon doctrine with Izanagi and Izanami (see Chapter 2); it also considered the Inner Shrine of Ise as corresponding to the womb mandala, and the Outer Shrine to the diamond mandala.[3]

The spiritual fervor of the Kamakura period (see Chapter 4) entailed not only the founding of new Buddhist sects but also an awakening of Shinto. Its adherents now advocated the "reverse theory of essence-manifestation." Placing the Shinto deities above the Buddhas and Bodhisattvas, they claimed that the *kami* deities were the original essence and that Buddhas and Bodhisattvas were the provisional manifestations of the *kami* essence. This shift in the balance of power between Buddhism and Shinto signaled the beginning of a move to articulate and systematize Shinto doctrines.

## The Emperor as Living *Kami*

The status of Shinto shrines was elevated in the mid-seventh century, under the patronage of Emperor Tenmu (r. 673–86) and Empress Jito (r. 686–97). It was Emperor Tenmu who ordered the compilation of the early Japanese history, which resulted in the *Kojiki* (712) and the *Nihongi* (720). He also offered imperial protection to major shrines, and in 674 he personally paid a visit to the Ise Shrine as his ancestor shrine. A religio-ideological move to identify the imperial family as the descendants of Amaterasu was then underway. The link between the reigning emperor or empress and Amaterasu was readily drawn, since ancient kings and queens had often been endowed with shamanic power and functioned as high priests and priestesses. Both Emperor Tenmu and Empress Jito were described by the court poets as living *kami*. This association between the imperial family and Shinto mythology would become the core ideology of Japanese nationalism; and as such it constitutes a sensitive issue for many Japanese today (see Chapters 7 and 8).

## A Divinely Protected Country

The confidence of the Shintoists was boosted by the Japanese victory over Mongol invading forces in 1274 and 1281. On both occasions, opportune typhoons swiftly and decisively sank the invaders' ships and killed many of their troops. The belief spread that Japan was protected by the *kami* deities, who would send a divine wind (*shinpu* or *kamikaze*) at times of national crisis. From then on, whenever

Japan came under threat by foreign powers, the typical response of the Japanese ruler would be to declare that "Japan is the country of *kami*."

This idea that Japan was a divinely protected country grew during the Muromachi period, based on the account of the unbroken line of the imperial succession since the "Age of the Gods." This view was brought to the fore by the learned warrior Kitabatake Chikafusa (1293–1354), a staunch supporter of the southern imperial court, during the period when Japan had two emperors, each claiming legitimacy (1336–92). In his *Records of the Legitimate Succession of the Divine Sovereigns* (*Jin'no shotoki,* 1339), Kitabatake declared: "Japan is the divine country [*shinkoku*]. The heavenly ancestor [i.e. the deity Kunitokotachi] it was who first laid its foundations, and the Sun Goddess left her descendants to reign over it forever and ever. This is true only of our country, and nothing similar may be found in foreign lands."[4] He borrowed from Confucianism to describe the moral virtues of the three regalia, the symbol of imperial authority: the mirror stood for honesty, the jewel for compassion (since it can sway and covers a wide area), and the sword for courage (as needed in making decisions). Kitabatake's attempt to give a systematic explanation to Shinto symbolism encouraged the further development of Shinto theology.

## The Emergence of Shinto Treatises

Kitabatake's claim had a textual basis in the works of Watarai Yukitada (1236–1305), a Shinto priest of the Outer Shrine of Ise. He described various facets of Shinto tradition, such as the history of *sengu* (see Chapter 2), and of Shinto symbolism, including the meaning of the evergreen *sakaki* (a sacred tree in Shinto because it is an example of something that fully receives the cosmic energy, or blessings of the *kami*, regardless of the season[5]).

Yoshida Kanetomo (1435–1511), head priest of the Yoshida Shrine in Kyoto, further developed Watarai's line of work. He asserted the primacy of Shinto over Buddhism by way of the "reverse essence-manifestation" theory. Yoshida took the example of a tree as a metaphor and explained that Shinto was the root and the trunk of all truth, Confucianism the branches and leaves, and Buddhism the fruit of the tree. He asserted that, in addition to the kinds of Shinto that had been amalgamated with Buddhism or woven into the esoteric Buddhist worldview, there was a pure, unadulterated core Shinto, a "primal Shinto," which was devoid of the influence of Confucianism, Buddhism, and Daoism.[6] Works by Watarai and Yoshida were early attempts to free Shinto from the yoke of Buddhism, and to assert its independence.

## Development of Popular Piety

The assertion that Shinto was an independent religion gave local Shinto shrines the impetus to gain more followers during the Muromachi period. The strategy of the Shinto clergy was to promote the message of longevity, health, military victory (to warriors), profits (to merchants), rich harvests (to peasants), and bounties (to fishermen)—all in exchange for their worshipping their *kami*. The accent was on "profit here and now" (*genze riyaku*). This idea appealed to people, and the popular belief in deities of good luck (*fukujin*) spread. Especially popular were the gods Ebisu (the god of fishing and commerce), Daikoku (the god of wealth, a kind of Japanese "Santa Claus"), and Bishamon (the god of wealth and power). Many of these deities are still revered today among those who make their living by fishing, farming, and commerce. In the spirit of "profit here and now," pilgrimage to the Ise Shrine also became extremely meritorious.[7]

# The Development of Kamakura Buddhist Sects

## Buddhist Sects in Arms

During the Sengoku period, when the entire country was divided into warlords' territories, the True Pure Land and Nichiren sects developed their own religious militias. The former found an organizational genius in the person of Ren'nyo (1415–99), who laid firm foundations for the sect's subsequent development. His followers established an independent territory, known as the "Ikko Ikki" (peasant revolt of the True Pure Land followers), which lasted from 1488 to 1580, and defended it with their own military forces. Nichiren's disciples also boasted strong-willed leaders. Among them was Nichijo (1298–1369), who was related by blood to the first Ashikaga shogun, Takauji, and won the coveted office of chaplain to the emperor. Various branches of the Nichiren sect gained large numbers of followers, and they organized a military unit following the Onin War (1467–77).

The True Pure Land and Nichiren sects often came into doctrinal conflict with other older establishments of Mt. Hiei and with the temples in Nara, which did not welcome the rapid growth of these newer Buddhist sects. By now, powerful older temples and monasteries had their own military units, made up of rambunctious "monk-soldiers" (*sohei*). Both the old and new Buddhist sects made pacts with warlords, who sided with the temples of their faith and who manipulated the temple forces to achieve their ends.

Because of its aggressive proselytizing, the Nichiren sect made itself an easy target of hostility. For instance, in 1469, Mt. Hiei pressured the shogunate to expel the followers of the Nichiren sects from the city of Kyoto; and the following year, the Kofukuji temple in Nara began its assault on the Nichirenites. In 1536, when the sponsors of the Nichiren sect publicly humiliated a monk from Mt. Hiei, who was giving a public talk on the teaching of the *Lotus Sutra*, Mt. Hiei monastery assembled its allies, mobilized a 60,000-strong army, and attacked the Nichiren temples in Kyoto. The Nichirenites, together with their allied warlords, defended their temples with a 20,000-strong army. After about a week of savage fighting all the Nichiren temples in Kyoto had been razed to the ground. The shogunate banned Nichiren priests from Kyoto, but lifted its ban six years later by petition of the followers of the Nichiren sects.[8]

## Doctrinal Debates

Not all the rivalry between sects involved violence, and the above example was in fact an exception. Doctrinal debates (*shuron*) had long been a fixture within the Japanese Buddhist tradition. For example, going back in time, Saicho had engaged in debates with a scholar-monk of the Nara school. During the fourteenth and the fifteenth centuries, debates among the new Buddhist sects were frequently held, and they typically involved the Nichiren sect. Perhaps precisely because the doctrinal debates were serious affairs in which the debaters staked their lives and the sects their honor, popular wisdom found it good material for satire. A **kyogen** play entitled *Doctrinal Debate (Shuron)*, exposes the silliness of petty sectarian rivalry. (*Kyogen* is a dramatic genre that is known for its democratic, witty, comical treatment of medieval social conflicts, often performed in between serious and somber noh plays as a kind of comic relief.) This piece was written in the fourteenth century and is still performed today. The storyline is as follows:

As the play opens, a Nichiren priest is returning to Kyoto from Mt. Minobu, having visited the temple where Nichiren had spent his last years; he is chanting "Namu Myoho-rengekyo" ("Homage to the marvelous *Lotus Sutra*"). There enters a Pure Land priest, chanting "Namu Amida-butsu." He is returning to Kyoto from a pilgrimage to the Zenkoji temple. Heading the same way, the two engage in friendly conversation; however, as soon as they find out that they belong to rival sects, they go their separate ways.

As darkness falls, one priest finds a roadside inn and settles there for the night. The other priest finds the same inn; and the innkeeper, seeing another priest on pilgrimage, assigns him to the same room as the first. The two exchange verbal insults (though without real malice and employing numerous puns), ridicule each other's doctrines, and attempt to convert each other. Eventually, fatigue overcomes them, and they go to bed. No sooner has the Nichiren priest fallen asleep, than the Pure Land priest gets up and begins his morning *nenbutsu* practice, shouting "Namu Amida-butsu" into the Nichiren priest's ear. The latter gets up to do his own morning chanting, and shouts the *mantra* "Namu Myoho-rengekyo" into the Pure Land priest's ear. Each excitedly takes up his wide-brimmed hat, beats on it to keep time, and begins to dance, while reciting his holy *mantra*. At the height of their frenzy, the two mix up their *mantras*; the Nichiren priest begins to shout, "Namu Amida-butsu," and the Pure Land priest shouts, "Namu Myoho-rengekyo"! When they realize what has happened, they look at each other, fall silent, then resume their dance, singing together: "The *Lotus Sutra* and Amida Buddha both bring about blessings to all sentient beings; be it the *Lotus* or Amida, there is no difference between the two. From now on, our names will be "Myo-Amida-Butsu" (the Marvelous Lotus-Amida Buddha). The two priests finish their dance, and then exit, followed by the innkeeper.[9]

It is remarkable that even violent religious conflicts could be turned into a source of laughter and diversion. This lighthearted attitude toward religion has always existed among the Japanese. A lady of the Heian court, Sei Shonagon, wrote, somewhat flippantly, that "A preacher ought to be good-looking. For if we are properly to understand his worthy sentiments, we must keep our eyes on him while he speaks; should we look away, we may forget to listen. Accordingly, an ugly preacher may well be the source of sin."[10]

## The Development of Zen Sects and the Zen-Influenced Arts

During the Muromachi period, the Rinzai and the Soto Zen sects made significant contributions to the cultural life of Japan. Five

Zen temples in Kamakura and five in Kyoto—the "five mountain" system initiated by the Kamakura Hojo regent—increasingly became centers of cultural activity. Although initially Soto masters were involved, because these five mountain temples were of the Rinzai sect, the latter received more prominence. (However it is perhaps erroneous even to speak of the influence of Zen upon Japanese culture in terms of the sectarian distinction between Rinzai and Soto.)

Zen aesthetic sensitivity, imbued with simplicity, depth, and minimalism, found expression in various art forms: ink painting (*suibokuga*), poetry (in Chinese), calligraphy, architecture, garden design, the tea ceremony, flower arrangement, and noh drama. The shogun Ashikaga Takauji embraced Zen Buddhism, just as the Hojo regents had done before him, and took Muso Kokushi (1275–1351) as his teacher.[11] After the death of Emperor Godaigo, Takauji wished to build a temple to comfort the emperor's departed soul and atone for his own sins of having ousted the emperor; he appointed Muso to carry out the conversion of an imperial villa into a temple, Tenryuji. Muso, a man of multiple talents and a gifted garden designer, was instrumental in the spread of a culture that was imbued with the spirit of Zen. Most of the Ashikaga shoguns were ardent patrons of Rinzai Zen, and their taste had a "trickling down" effect, coloring the entire Muromachi culture with Zen aesthetics.

The Soto Zen sect began to expand under the able leadership of Keizan Jokin (1264–1325), who discarded the purist attitude of its founder, Dogen, admitted lay practitioners, and incorporated esoteric rituals. Keizan was a gifted teacher and trained outstanding disciples, who, together with the master, energetically established temples throughout the Hokuriku region, including the great Sojiji temple, the second most important temple of the Soto sect. They also proselytized actively, gaining a huge number of followers.

Among the artists who came under the influence of Soto Zen was Zeami Motokiyo (1363–1443), a great noh playwright, performer, and thinker. Following in the footsteps of his father, Kan'ami, Zeami fundamentally gave shape to noh drama, elevating it from folk entertainment into an art. Zeami studied Zen under Master Chikuso Chigen, abbot of Hoganji temple, in Yamato. This Soto Zen temple was the first to be built in the Yamato region and belonged to the Sojiji line.[12] Taking the Zen teaching of an open mental attitude, which goes beyond the egocentric subject–object dichotomy, as the basis of his performing theory, Zeami placed great importance on the constant

**IN FOCUS**

# The Japanese Garden

THE HISTORY OF THE JAPANESE GARDEN, which goes back to antiquity, reflects the history of Japanese religion itself. A consecrated plot of land (*saniwa*), marked off and covered by small, smooth stones, was the sacred space where an emperor (or empress) would sit and perform on a stringed instrument in order to summon the spirit of the *kami*, who would deliver an oracle, which the prime minister, also present, was to interpret. This consecrated ground is one of the components of later Japanese gardens.

The art of garden making, developed in China and Korea, was introduced into Japan by Korean immigrants around the time Buddhism was introduced. On their estates, clan chiefs built gardens containing man-made ponds and islands, depicting Horai, the island of the immortals according to Daoist legend, or Mt. Sumeru, the center of the universe according to Buddhist cosmology.

During the Heian period gardens became more elaborate. The mansions of aristocrats became the setting for water gardens, which would consist of a large but shallow artificial lake, or series of ponds, containing islands, waterfalls, and bridges. Chinese *fengshui* principles were observed in arranging the stream, stones, and trees in the garden.

From the eleventh century onward, under the influence of Pure Land Buddhism, gardens aimed to replicate the Paradise of Amida Buddha, taking from the descriptions in Buddhist *sutras*. The Byodoin Temple in Uji is a fine example of a paradise garden. The gilded statue of Amida Buddha, honorably placed in the main hall of the temple building, is reflected in the garden pond. At night the image of the Buddha is lit; its reflection in the water creates a mysterious atmosphere.

In the fourteenth century, under the influence of Zen Buddhism, gardens took on an entirely different look. Zen gardens tended to be smaller, because they were often built behind the main hall of a temple, as a private space rather than a public arena. Along with professional garden designers some talented Zen monks designed gardens, typically adopting a minimalist approach. Landscapes, often depicted without using water (known as the "dry garden," or *karesansui*), became popular.

The most celebrated garden of the latter kind is the rock garden of the Ryoanji temple. Fifteen rocks of varying size drift in twos and threes atop

*The starkly abstract rock garden at Ryoanji temple, Kyoto. Gardens such as this reflect the aesthetic cultivated by Zen Buddhist meditation.*

a "sea" of white gravel. Because of its simplicity, numerous attempts have been made to explain the "meaning" of the garden, but the statement made by the rocks seems to transcend any such attempt. Wrapped in a pregnant silence, Zen gardens such as this are popular as places for meditation, where one may enjoy a moment of tranquility.

During the Azuchi-Momoyama period, which saw a celebration of secular over religious values, gardens became ornate, and unusal stones and showy plants were favored. Most Japanese gardens today are of a mixed style, consciously adopting various techniques to enhance the limited garden space. These include the practice of incorporating the natural landscape that forms the background of a garden as part of its design— a technique called "borrowing the view."

Japanese garden designers have always found individuality in rocks. After all, no two natural rocks are identical in shape, color, or texture. And yet, rocks possess the quality of stability and something of an animistic presence; in olden days, the *kami* deities were believed to descend into them. This lingering sentiment explains the special locution employed by Japanese gardeners: they do not speak of "placing" or "arranging" rocks, but rather of "erecting" and "assembling." When they move a rock—even with a mechanical device—they call the process "walking the rock." A rock is typically buried with two-thirds of its volume below the surface, and only its "head" showing. This "grounds" the rock.

While the comfort and sense of healing and peace we gain from a garden are universal, a Japanese garden, with its subtle philosophical principles, adds an extra dimension to our appreciation.

diligent practice of the performer—reflecting Dogen's philosophy of the religious life as one of constant practice. Zeami's theory of performance was deeply imbued with the Zen awareness of subject–object unity.

## Francis Xavier and the Introduction of Christianity

The arrival of the first Christian missionaries in Japan, in 1549, could not have been more opportunely timed. In the mid-sixteenth century Japan was embroiled in civil war; and in an age of "conquer or be conquered," the warlords (*daimyo*) had discarded many old beliefs and superstitions. Pragmatism, rationality, and well-calculated ruthless military strategies began to emerge. The medieval Japanese religion-centered worldview was gradually disappearing amidst the war cries of soldiers, the sound of horses' hooves, and the echoes of gunfire (guns having recently been introduced to Japan by Portuguese sailors).

The global expansion of Christianity must be placed within the context of contemporary European scientific discoveries (such as Toscanelli's map based on the view that the earth is round, and Copernicus' and Kepler's discovery that the earth revolves around the sun), the advancement of navigation skills and technology (promoted by Prince Henry the Navigator of Portugal), and the spirit of exploration of ocean routes (carried out by Vasco Da Gama, Columbus, and Magellan). The Protestant Reformation, initiated in 1517 by Martin Luther, and the Roman Catholic Counter-Reformation that followed, added another dimension to this picture. It was in this dynamic, colorful, and exciting period of global history that the introduction of Christianity into Japan took place.

Born into a distinguished family in Navarre, northern Spain, Francis Xavier (1506–52) was one of the founding members of the Society of Jesus, or Jesuits.[13] One of the order's missions was to convert "pagans" to Christianity. Xavier was posted to Goa in India, where he proselytized for several years, during which time he came to meet Anjiro, a Japanese convict taking refuge overseas. Xavier became Anjiro's confessor and the latter was converted to Catholicism. As he got to know Anjiro, Xavier became convinced that he should proselytize in Japan. He and two other Jesuits, Father Cosme de Torres and Brother Juan Fernández, accompanied by Anjiro who acted as an interpreter, set sail from Goa and arrived at Kagoshima on August 15, 1549. Xavier's first impression of the Japanese, reported to the Jesuits' office in Goa, was favorable:

> The people with whom we have thus far conversed are the best that we have yet discovered; and it seems to me that, among pagan nations, there will not be another to surpass the Japanese. They are a race of very fine manners and generally good and not malicious, a people of an astonishingly great sense of honor, who prize honor more than any other thing.[14]

## Initial Obstacles

The first major obstacle for Xavier and his company was the language. With the help of Anjiro, Xavier soon learned enough rudimentary Japanese to recite the Ten Commandments, and Brother Fernández turned out to be a gifted linguist. Together, they translated the catechism into Japanese.

Xavier and his company condemned as "evil" certain customs that they found in Japan, especially the corrupt lifestyle of monks and nuns within the monasteries, the prevalent male homosexual practices, and the practice of women aborting children or killing newborn babies when they could not afford to rear them.[15] Surprisingly, their criticisms won the support of socially concerned Japanese, as well as of those already inclined to be critical of Buddhist institutions.

The major doctrinal hurdle for the Japanese was the Jesuits' insistence that only Christians could achieve salvation. Although interested in Christian teaching (which they initially took to be another version of Buddhism from India), the Japanese could not accept the idea that their ancestors, who had no way of knowing Christian teachings, were condemned to eternal hellfire.

Xavier knew the legend of St. Thomas the Apostle, whereby St. Thomas had crossed the Arabian Sea, reaching India and beyond, and had converted the people of Asia to Christianity. Xavier hoped that this legend might just turn out to be applicable to Japan. In his discussion with learned Buddhist priests (of the Shingon sect), he was heartened to find that they agreed with the notion of an omnipotent, omnipresent, and omniscient God—a notion akin to their understanding of the Buddha essence: the cosmic Buddha, or Mahavairochana. A few days later, however, when Xavier described to them the idea of God the Creator and the immortality of the soul, he learned that these ideas were foreign to Japanese priests, for they saw all phenomena as constantly arising and disappearing. When it came to doctrines of Christ's incarnation and Resurrection and of the Trinity, the priests rejected them as "dreams and fables."[16]

Despite these theological difficulties, Xavier was a man of humility and sincerity, and his nobility of manner and devotion to his faith won the hearts of those Japanese who came in contact with him. Warlords, intellectuals, and highborn ladies all began to show interest in the Christian message he conveyed. In Yamaguchi, where Xavier stayed for a time, the local warlord gave him an abandoned Buddhist temple for use as a church. Xavier and his company also introduced European scientific knowledge to the Japanese, which greatly enhanced their credibility. Xavier reported to his superiors:

> The Japanese . . . do not know that the earth is round, nor
> do they know the course of the sun; and they ask about
> these things and others such as how comets, lightning, rain,
> and snow, and similar things are produced. We answer and
> explain these to them, and they were very happy and
> content and regarded us as learned men, which was no little
> help in their giving credence to our words.[17]

Xavier's mission was a modest success. He left Japan for China in 1551, leaving his companions behind. Soon afterward, however, his health deteriorated rapidly, and he died in Macao on December 3, 1552. He was beatified on October 25, 1619, and canonized on March 12, 1622, by Pope Gregory XV. To this day, the people of Yamaguchi take pride in having welcomed this noble saint into their midst, more than four centuries ago, and even non-Christian taxi drivers will talk endearingly of their town's adopted son.

## Nobunaga and Christianity

In his campaign to unify Japan, the warlord Oda Nobunaga faced considerable opposition from the militarily armed True Pure Land community of Ishiyama Honganji, near Osaka. His frustration at the Buddhist establishment was directed against Mt. Hiei, the powerful and well-armed monastic center. In 1571, Nobunaga attacked Mt. Hiei, slaughtering anyone in the way of his army, and razing all the temple buildings, which numbered over a thousand. Two years later, he seized Kyoto, putting an end to the Ashikaga shogunate.

Out of his antipathy for Buddhist sects, Nobunaga patronized Christianity, using it as a counterweight to Buddhist political power; Christianity thus gained powerful backing and enjoyed privileges for the next fifty years. In 1576, the first Christian church, Nan-banji (literally, "Western Temple"), was erected in Kyoto. By 1580 there were 150,000 Japanese Christians (or *kirishitan*), and in Kyoto alone there were more than 200 chapels.[18] The Visitor-General of the Jesuit order, Alessandro Valignano, who came to Japan three times (1579–82, 1590–92, and 1598–1603), did much to promote Christianity in Japan. He was an able administrator, who received permission from Nobunaga to build Christian schools and seminaries. Valignano was also a man of cross-cultural awareness, who saw the importance of understanding Japanese culture and accommodating Japanese customs in order to spread Christianity. He also recommended that a Japanese envoy be sent to the Vatican. A group of four young men, sponsored by the Japanese Christian warlords, set off for Rome in 1582, accompanied by Valignano. After a long and perilous voyage, the envoy arrived in Lisbon in 1584; from there, via Madrid, they traveled to Italy and entered Rome from Florence. In February 1585 they were granted an audience with the 84-year-old Pope Gregory XIII. Their visit greatly gladdened the pope, who embraced them warmly.

## Hideyoshi and Christianity

Nobunaga's successor, Toyotomi Hideyoshi, initially adopted Nobunaga's political and military agenda; he also extended the same favorable treatment to the Jesuits. For a while, Western-style clothes imported by Portuguese merchants were the object of great curiosity, and some even secretly tried tasting beef (the slaughtering of four-legged animals for food had traditionally been forbidden by the Buddhist injunction against taking life). This open-armed welcome of things Western did not last long, however. The Westerners forced people to convert, openly ate meat, and even sold Japanese children and women to the overseas slave market.[19] Local warlords donated real estate to the Church, including the port of Nagasaki. Japanese converts sometimes attacked and destroyed Buddhist temples and Shinto shrines.

Then on July 25, 1587, out of the blue, Hideyoshi published an edict banning Christianity and ordering missionaries (but not the Portuguese merchants) to quit Japan within twenty days.[20] In this edict, Hideyoshi reverted to the age-old rhetoric that Japan was the

*The first Christian missionaries arrived in Japan in 1549. The costumes and customs of the Europeans, and their exotic animals and imports, were objects of fascination for the Japanese.*

"divine country" (*shinkoku*). The first two articles of the edict read: "It is deplorable that Christians introduced their teachings to Japan, the divine country"; "It is unheard of that missionaries should force people to convert to their faith and incite them to demolish shrines and temples."[21] However, this edict was only a formal warning, and the Jesuits continued their missionary activities.

Valignano's second visit to Japan, in 1590, eased Hideyoshi's anxiety, and Christianity continued to flourish. Sometime in 1592 or 1593, the Spanish entered into trade with Japan. Spain dispatched a Dominican priest, as well as several Franciscans, as "ambassadors." The Jesuits and Portuguese, who had hitherto enjoyed the monopoly of evangelizing and trade, respectively, were disturbed by these events. Rivalries among the Jesuits, the Dominicans, and the Franciscans, exacerbated by their nations' conflicts over profits gained from their overseas trade, would eventually lead to their total expulsion from Japan.

## The Incident of the *San Felipe* and the Christian Martyrs

The favoritism extended to the Christians came to an abrupt end in 1596, when a Spanish galleon, the *San Felipe*, caught in a typhoon off the coast of Tosa, drifted almost ashore. The ship was confiscated by the local authority, and those on board were questioned. The captain of the *San Felipe* produced a map of the world, on which two lines were drawn, dividing the globe into the areas under Spanish control and those under Portuguese control—a division first declared by Pope Alexander VI in 1493, and modified in 1494 and 1529. The pilot pointed out the vast extent of the dominions of the Spanish king, Philip II, and told the Japanese official: "Our Kings begin by sending into the countries they wish to conquer priests who induce the people to embrace our religion, and when they have made considerable progress, troops are sent who combine with the new Christians, and then our Kings have not much trouble in accomplishing the rest."[22]

This incident gave Hideyoshi a sufficient reason to ban Christianity. Signs of colonization by the Western powers were evident in Asia; he needed only to look at Macao and the Philippines. When Franciscans, now forbidden to enter Japan, smuggled themselves in and were subsequently discovered, Hideyoshi's anger erupted. They were arrested, paraded from Kyoto to Nagasaki on foot, and crucified, according to methods developed by the Office of the Inquisition. Twenty-six Christians—Franciscan missionaries and Japanese converts—were burnt at the stake in Nagasaki on February 5, 1597, becoming the first Christian martyrs in Japan. (These twenty-six men were later canonized.)

## Deification of Hideyoshi

Hideyoshi died in 1598. In compliance with his will, the Toyokuni Shrine was built in 1599 in the Higashiyama district of Kyoto, which venerated his spirit as a *kami*. Hideyoshi had been a generous patron of the imperial family and had lavishly sponsored the forty-first *sengu*—rebuilding of the Ise Shrine buildings—in 1585.[23] In gratitude, the imperial court granted him the posthumous title of "Toyokuni **Daimyojin**" (the Great Deity, Toyokuni, the Wealth of the Nation).

**IN FOCUS**

## The Way of Tea and Zen

IN ESSENCE, THE JAPANESE "tea ceremony," or *chanoyu*, is quite simple. Guests are invited to have some tea. The host pours some hot water into a tea bowl and whisks the powdered green tea to dissolve it. The host then offers tea to each guest; guests drink the tea in a few sips, and afterwards appreciate the fine tea bowl. Sweets may be served to counterbalance the bitter taste of the tea.

Powdered green tea, simmering hot water, a tea bowl, a bamboo ladle, a small powder scoop, and a bamboo whisk—that is all one needs to make a bowl of tea; or is it? What makes *chanoyu* (literally, "tea hot water") an art is the mental and spiritual attitude that one brings to it, whether one is a host or a guest. Over a bowl of tea, host and guest(s) relish quiet, intimate moments together. Beneath the rigidly controlled appearance, the essence of *chanoyu* is actually the art of entertainment, private and spiritually refined.

During the Muromachi period, the making and serving of tea in an elaborate style at formal gatherings became fashionable among the nobles and warlords. In this palatial style of tea ceremony, gold, silver, and ivory utensils were used. Countering this trend, Murato Shuko (or Juko, 1422–1502) created a new, simpler style of *chanoyu*, inspired by his practice of Zen under Master Ikkyu Sojun (1394–1481). Ikkyu was abbot of the Daitokuji temple in Kyoto, a gifted poet, and widely respected among the artistically minded. His disciples formed a small artistic and intellectual circle—what in the West might be called a "salon." Shuko must have learned from Ikkyu the monastic style of tea preparation and surmised the possibility of bringing it together with Zen spirituality. Shuko is today revered as the founder of the "Way of tea"; he removed ostentatious glitter from the palatial *chanoyu* and laid down the rules for a simple ceremony.

To begin with, "small talk" has no place in the tea ceremony. Guests shed the "dust of the world," as they enter the tea room from the garden. In Shuko's time, this "dust of the world" included class distinctions. He advised his students to cultivate an egalitarian mind by "respecting the lowly and being indifferent to titles." Another important piece of advice from Shuko was to cultivate cleanliness "both inside and outside." The pure mind that is needed for tea preparation was ultimately nothing other than the immaculate, blissful buddha-mind, which is free of ratiocination, or calculations of gain and loss. The "tea mind" is honest, sincere, and compassionate.

Shuko's disciple Takeno Joo (1504–55) handed down this art to Sen no Rikyu (1522–90), who further reduced the art to its bare essentials. He designed a tea room containing only two *tatami* mats in an alcove, and removed all decorations save a simple flower arrangement. Rikyu's style of tea is known as *wabi-cha*. "Wabi" means "minimalist" in today's parlance—it is the elegance of simplicity, of deliberate understatement. Instead of bright colors, muted colors were favored; for the tea bowl, for instance, black was preferred to red. Rikyu was an accomplished connoisseur of *objets d'art* and a fine artist; he served both Oda Nobunaga and Toyotomi Hideyoshi as tea master.

An anecdote known as "Rikyu's morning glory gathering" illustrates something of his greatness. Early one morning, Hideyoshi rushed to Rikyu's garden to see the morning glories that he heard were splendidly in bloom. When he got there, however, he saw not a single flower. Displeased, he entered the small tea room, where he found "a single morning glory of deep tinge displayed in the alcove." To cut off and remove all but one of the morning glories blooming in the garden would seem to most people a heartless thing to do, but Rikyu's aesthetic focused on the metaphysical principle. He wanted to show the beauty of morning glories in that *one* particular morning glory. In a single morning glory, all the morning glories are contained. To see oneness in the multitude and the multitude in oneness is a perception cultivated by Buddhists, not unlike the mystical awareness expressed by William Blake: "To see a World in a Grain of Sand/And a Heaven in a Wild flower" (*Auguries of Innocence*). This kind of spiritual awareness sustains the art of tea.

Today, tea masters speak of "harmony" (*wa*), "reverence" (*kei*), "purity" (*sei*), and "tranquility" (*jaku*) as the guiding spirit of *chanoyu*. An accomplished aesthete-philosopher, Yanagi Muneyoshi (1889–1961), poignantly captured the religious aspect of *chanoyu* in these words: "The way of tea is a way of salvation through beauty . . . Insofar as *chanoyu* is a Way, spiritual discipline should come first."

## Ieyasu and the Tokugawa Shogunate

With the establishment of the Tokugawa shogunate at Edo (Tokyo) in 1603, the expansive spirit of the preceding era gradually disappeared as the shogunate adopted strict measures to control all aspects of people's lives and institutions. The warlords, now granted the title of feudal  lords, pledged their absolute loyalty to the shogunate and headed their provinces. It was the shogunate's paramount concern to maintain domestic peace, and the government issued numerous regulations and orders to achieve this end.

Tokugawa Ieyasu was inclined to prohibit Christianity, although he had mixed feelings about Westerners. In 1600 a Dutch ship had drifted to the coast of Japan, carrying a few Dutch and English men of learning. Impressed by the caliber of these men, Ieyasu had warmly welcomed them and gave the Dutch permission to trade with Japan. He took the Englishman Will Adams (1564–1620) as an advisor. Later, however—in 1612—Ieyasu banned Christianity. The shogunate officials were concerned about two things: one was the fear of Western countries taking over Japan, and the other was that Japanese Christians might unite themselves across the social classes and so become a social force that would challenge the foundation of the new shogunate. Although a class system had always existed in Japanese society, by this time a rigid division of classes into "samurai, peasants, artisans, and merchants" had taken shape (aristocrats and clerics were apparently classes of their own).

The rivalry between Protestant countries (the Netherlands and England) and Catholic ones (Spain and Portugal) added to the complications, as they brought to the shogunate accusations concerning one another's wrongdoings on the sea and in their trade practices.

## The Isolationist Policy

In 1614 and 1615, the Tokugawa shogunate launched its final attack on the Toyotomi; at that time Western Christian missionaries and Japanese Christians sided with the Toyotomi and rallied against the shogunate's anti-Christianity policy. This unnerved the shogunate, and following the conclusion of the battle, the shogunate stepped up its prohibition of Christianity. But Christian missionaries continued to smuggle themselves into Japan on merchant ships. The best way to stop that was to stop trading, and in 1624 the shogunate refused any further trade with Spain; in 1635, it established the office of "temple and shrine police" (*jisha bugyo*). Systematic arrest and torture of Christians also began.

Peasants in the Shimabara region near Nagasaki had been suffering from poor harvests since 1634, and additionally from the ruthless taxes collected by the local lord. In 1637, their frustration erupted into a peasant uprising, which quickly spread to the neighboring island of Amakusa. Shimabara and Amakusa were areas formerly heavily populated by Japanese Christians.[1] This insurrection was suppressed the following year by shogunate forces, but it gave the shogunate the perfect excuse to ban Christianity altogether. In 1639 it forbade Portuguese merchants from entering Japanese ports. The closure of the Japanese ports—other than to Dutch and Chinese merchants and Korean diplomats—was thus completed. In 1641 the shogunate moved the Dutch commercial base to the man-made island of Dejima in Nagasaki so that the comings and going of Europeans could be monitored. For the next 200 years, no Christian missionary would be allowed into Japan.

## Persecution of Christians and the Formation of the *Danka* System

As early as 1614, the shogunate had ordered Buddhist temples to issue a "certificate of apostasy" to Christians who renounced their faith. The Christians had no choice but to renounce if they wanted to keep their heads on their shoulders. After the Shimabara Rebellion, the shogunate tightened up the practice of "examination of religious affiliations" (*shumon aratame*). Every Japanese family (*ie*), as a unit, was required to have the local Buddhist temple issue a certificate testifying that they were *not* Christians. In order to obtain this certificate, a family was obliged to become a patron (*danka*) of a Buddhist temple. This grew into a system known as the **"danka" system**, which was the direct outcome of the prohibition of Christianity. Each village head gathered these temple registrations and submitted them to the local lord. On Kyushu, where Christianity had taken deep root, people were required to prove their innocence by stamping on a wooden or metal plaque that bore the holy picture of the *Pietà*, the Crucifixion, or other Christian images. This screening practice was known as *fumie* (literally, "picture-stamping"), and became part of the annual New Year rituals for the citizens of Nagasaki. Christianity was totally prohibited, and resistant Christians were persecuted. Those who kept their Christian faith had to do so secretly as "crypto-Christians" (***kakure kirishitan***).

The shogunate's ruthless persecution of Christians proved to be extremely efficient. A German scientist, Engelbert Kaempfer, who visited Japan in 1690 as a member of the Dutch trade mission to Japan, recorded in his report home that Christianity had once been hugely successful in Japan, owing to the tireless effort of the Western missionaries, and that Japan had been on the brink of turning into a Christian country. However, he noted how "the ambitious views and impatient endeavors" of the Spanish and Portuguese missionaries to "reap the temporal as well as the spiritual fruits of their care and labor" had provoked the shogunate to launch "a persecution, which had not its parallel in history, whereby the religion they preached, and those who professed it, were in a few years time entirely exterminated."[2]

## The Deification of Ieyasu

When Ieyasu died in 1616, the shogunate saw fit that he, too, be deified and worshipped as a *kami*, just as Hideyoshi had been. A Tendai priest, Tenkai, an advisor on religious and political matters who had worked closely with Ieyasu, insisted on the posthumous title of "**Daigongen**" (great incarnation of the buddha essence) for Ieyasu. In 1635, the third shogun and grandson of Ieyasu, Iemitsu (r. 1613–51), built an elaborate mausoleum for Ieyasu on the mountain of Nikko, which had been a sacred site for mountain ascetics since ancient times. Ten years later, the posthumous title of "Tosho Daigongen" (Great Buddha Incarnate as the Sun God of the East) was granted to Ieyasu by the imperial court. The Nikko mausoleum soon became a popular pilgrimage site. The splendor of its ornate Yomei Gate and of other buildings in the compound became famed far and wide as things one must see in order to believe their grandeur.

## The Obaku Zen Sect

The port of Nagasaki remained accessible to the Chinese. In 1654, upon the ardent invitation of a Zen priest in Nagasaki, Ingen Ryuki (1592–1673), a 62-year-old Chan master of the Wanfusi (Manpukuji in Japanese) monastery at Mt. Huangbo (Obaku in Japanese), crossed the sea to Japan from Qing China, accompanied by some thirty disciples. Ingen was a master of the highest caliber, erudite and enlightened, and widely sought out by Chan monasteries throughout China. He had initially intended to stay in Japan for three years only and return to his disciples in China. The fourth shogun, Ietsuna (r. 1651–80), having heard of this great Chinese Zen master, gave him a special audience. Impressed by Ingen, Ietsuna made him a gift of some land in Uji, south of Kyoto, where he could build a monastery. Seeing this as his destiny, Ingen made his permanent home in Japan. In 1661, he established the monastery of Manpukuji, named after his home monastery in China; it was built in a beautiful Ming style with brightly colored pillars and splendid calligraphy adorning the buildings. Thus, Ingen became the founder of the Japanese **Obaku** sect of Zen, which combined *zazen* and *nenbutsu* practices—a hybrid style of devotion then widespread in Chinese Chan monasteries. Japanese Zen monks, thirsty for new knowledge and renewed practice, flocked to Manpukuji to train under Ingen, regardless of their Rinzai or Soto sectarian affiliation. Many feudal lords, courtiers, and high-ranking samurai also sought to be associated with him.[3]

As a "latecomer" to the world of Japanese Zen, the Obaku sect never gained prominence, but it has enjoyed unique prestige, thanks to the extraordinary personality of its founder. Today, the followers of the Obaku sect number some 350,000, about 8.5 percent of all Zen followers.

## Buddhism Under the Shogunate

The "danka" system—in which every family was obliged to become a patron of a local temple in order to prove that they were not Christians—turned Buddhist temples into a formally established institution. By 1660, Buddhist temples received the unquestioning support of the people. Each patron was required to contribute to the priest's living expenses and to share any cost of building or repairing temple buildings. Everyone was required to attend the temple ceremonies, which commemorated the founder of the temple, the day of the Buddha's death, and so forth. During the midsummer *bon* period, when the ancestors' spirits were believed to return for a brief reunion with the living, visits to ancestral graves kept in the temple grounds were obligatory. So were such visits during the spring and autumn equinox periods.

In this way, the temple became the hub of people's annual religious rituals. Its financial stability was more than assured; in fact, in 1665 the shogunate had to issue an order, "Regulations for the Buddhist Sects and Temples" (*Shoshu jiin hatto*) to curtail the luxurious lifestyle enjoyed by Buddhist temple priests. Taking advantage of this, some feudal lords who were hostile to Buddhist temples closed down temples that did not comply with the order.[4]

## Buddhism Becomes a Funeral Religion

By 1700 the *danka* system was firmly in place. Temples compiled a "family history" for each household, obliged each household to erect a gravestone, and expanded their land holdings to accommodate these. Buddhism turned into a funeral religion which centered upon memorial services for ancestors (*senzo kuyo*). Buddhist priests thus found themselves the caretakers of the dead.

Every household had to observe the "thirteen commemorative rituals for the dead," each of which had to be conducted by a Buddhist priest. These memorial services were offered on the seventh day, the twenty-seventh day, the thirty-seventh day, the forty-seventh day, the fifty-seventh day, the sixty-seventh day, the seventy-ninth day, and the one-hundredth day, as well as the first anniversary, the third anniversary, the seventh anniversary, the thirteenth anniversary, and finally, the thirty-third anniversary of the death.[5]

As cumbersome as their scheduling may seem, these memorial rituals are faithfully observed in Japan even to this day, although in a much abbreviated fashion. During the Edo period, for a family not to observe these rituals raised the authorities' suspicions that members of the family might be crypto-Christian or followers of the forbidden Nichiren sub-sect of *Fujufuse*. The Fujufuse sect was exclusively sectarian, refusing to provide religious services for non-followers or acknowledge their sponsorship. The sect refused to comply with the political authorities, and that was reason enough for the shogunate to suppress it.

# The Spread of Confucian Learning

Even before the Edo period, the study of Song Neo-Confucianism, especially the teachings of Zhu Xi (1130–1200, Shushi in Japanese), had attracted the attention of warlords and high-ranking samurai. The Neo-Confucian teachings of moral life and its application to statecraft appealed to them. But it was during the Edo period that the teachings of Neo-Confucianism blossomed into an important religious and ethical force. Neo-Confucians embraced self-cultivation and "the investigation of things"—the objective study of things around them—as essential doctrines. Neo-Confucianism taught that individual persons, through their engagement in objective rational reflection, were able to transform their individual nature, deluded by selfishness and desires, into pure human nature, which partook of the cosmic principle of the highest moral good. The unity and harmony of the microcosm (human persons) and the macrocosm (the universe), or the individual, the state, and heaven and earth, was, by virtue of shared morality, the core-intuition of Neo-Confucianism. Zhu Xi taught that this principle (*li* in Chinese, *ri* in Japanese) is activated by the material force (*qi* in Chinese, *ki* in Japanese) in each individual.[6]

Japanese Neo-Confucian scholars modified the Chinese doctrines to suit their own situation. Chinese Neo-Confucians emphasized both the individual in relation to the universe and the practice of statecraft, and upheld that an individual, by transforming his human nature, could commune with the cosmic moral principle. By contrast, Japanese Confucians tended to focus on the social relationships and obligations of the individual.[7] Zhu Xi had taught that individuals were born unequal due to different material forces, and this appealed to the Japanese Confucians as providing the rationale for a class-based society.[8] Statements such as these reflected widely held beliefs: "The samurai are superior to the common people; it is thus natural that the samurai rule," and "Peasants produce the five grains and as such they are the basis of the country; artisans create tools; but merchants just exchange what others produce in order to gain profit, and therefore they are of the lowest class."[9]

The increasing interest in Neo-Confucianism was in part fueled by a rising tide of anti-Buddhist feeling. For instance, the lords of Okayama, Aizu, and Mito provinces all embraced Confucianism in their dislike of Buddhism. Also, the Neo-Confucian scholar employed by the shogunate, Hayashi Razan (1583–1657), deeply resented the

Buddhist priests, Tenkai (1536–1643) and Suden (1569–1633), who acted as Ieyasu's close advisors. But the overall prevailing attitude toward Neo-Confucianism was one of inclusion. In 1690, the fifth shogun, Tsunayoshi (r. 1680–1709), himself a dedicated patron of Buddhism, established the Sacred Hall for Confucian studies, the Shohei School, at Yushima, in Edo. By the end of the seventeenth century, Confucian learning had gained the official support of the shogunate and had grown into an influential intellectual and moral trend.

Some Japanese Confucian scholars rejected the lofty idealism of Zhu Xi in favor of the teaching of Wang Yangming (1472–1529; O Yomei in Japanese). While making room for human weaknesses, Wang Yangming advocated the cosmic unity of Heaven, Earth, and men, and emphasized the unity of words and deeds as the ethical goal. Nakae Toju (1608–48), the founder of the Japanese O Yomei School, led an exemplary life and came to be known as the "sage of Omi Province." Still other Japanese Confucians turned their attention directly to the teachings of Confucius (551–479 B.C.E.) and Mencius (371–289? B.C.E.), bypassing the interpretations offered by Zhu Xi. This school of **Kogaku** (Ancient Learning), led by Ito Jinsai (1625–1705) and his son, Ito Togai (1670–1736), had numerous followers in Kyoto.

## The Fusion of Shinto and Confucianism

Some Confucians found in Shinto a natural ally, because both Shinto and Neo-Confucianism emphasized the importance of sincerity of heart and the individual as an integral part of heaven and earth (or nature).[10] The most notable example of the Shinto–Neo-Confucianism synthesis was the thought developed by Yamasaki Ansai (1618–82), an accomplished Neo-Confucian scholar. He befriended Watarai Nobuyoshi (1615–90), a Shinto priest of the Ise Shrine, and Yoshikawa (or Kikkawa) Koretaru (1615–94), who headed the Yoshida Shrine in Kyoto,[11] came under the influence of Shinto, and was initiated into the methods of Shinto purification rituals.

Ansai was convinced that the principle (or the Way) of the Neo-Confucians was also present in pure Shinto.[12] For him, the essence of Neo-Confucian teaching of "unswerving loyalty and selflessness, guarded by an ever-vigilant mind" was contained in Princess Yamato's prophecy: "For the *kami* to come down (*sui*), you need first of all prayers; to receive blessings (*myo-ga*), you need straightforwardness, and if thus you gain the Great Way, the realm will prosper in peace."[13] In 1671, in recognition of this insight, Yoshikawa Koretaru gave Ansai the Shinto name "Suika," derived from the prophecy itself: "sui" (to come down) and "ga" (also pronounced "ka"; increase of divine blessings). Ansai, now revered as a living *kami*, became the head priest of his own sect, Suika Shinto, which attracted 6,000 disciples, who were also learned students of Neo-Confucianism.[14]

Shinto steadily gained importance during the Edo period. An agricultural reformer and sage, Ninomiya Sontoku (1787–1856), embraced Buddhism, Confucianism, and Shinto, maintaining that "Shinto is the way which provides the foundation of the country; Confucianism is the way which provides for governing the country; and Buddhism is the way which provides for governing one's mind." He recommended a "pill" made up of half Shinto, one-quarter Confucianism, and one-quarter Buddhism as the ideal spiritual dosage.[15]

## The Poet Basho

Even in the regulation-bound feudal society, the essential freedom of the human spirit could not be completely suppressed. The great haiku master Matsuo Basho (1644–94) bears witness to this. Born into a minor samurai family, he renounced this life in his early twenties to become a poet, and took "Basho" (banana tree) as his pen name. He was a contradiction of everything the shogunate tried to implement by way of strict regulations. For a time, he was a student of Zen; and this may have influenced his outlook on life. He chose traveling as a way of nurturing and sharpening his poetic creativity, and fondly visited famous shrines and temples. In the early autumn of 1684, he traveled to Ise and recorded his impression of the place:

> I visited the outer shrine of Ise one evening just before dark. The first gate of the shrine was standing in the shadow, and the lights were glimmering in the background. As I stood there, lending my ears to the roar of pine trees upon distant mountains, I felt moved deep in the bottom of my heart.
> > In the utter darkness
> > Of a moonless night,
> > A powerful wind embraces
> > The ancient cedar trees.
> I do not wear a single piece of metal on my belt, nor do I carry anything but a sack on my shoulder. My head is clean-

shaven, and I have a string of beads in my hand. I am indeed dressed like a priest, but priest I am not, for the dust of the world still clings to me. The keeper of the inner shrine prevented me from entering the holy seat of the god[dess] because my appearance was like that of a Buddhist priest.[16]

This custom of prohibiting Buddhist priests from entering the sanctuary at Ise goes back a long time. A similar account by a monk, Muju Ichinen (1226–1312), survives. He noted that at the Ise Shrine, "words associated with the three treasures of Buddhism were forbidden at the shrine" and that "monks could not closely approach the sacred buildings."[17] In fact, the imperial princesses who served as priestesses at Ise had to avoid certain taboo words, such as "childbirth," "illness," and "death," as well as "tears" and "blood"; also included in the list were words having to do with Buddhism, such as "Buddha," "*sutra*," "monk," and "nun." Instead of "Buddha," the priestess used the words, "the middle child" (possibly because the Buddha figure was depicted flanked by bodhisattvas on both sides); the *sutras* were called "dyed paper" (because Buddhist *sutras* were written on fancy paper dyed with plant dyes on which occasionally gold and silver powders were sprinkled), and monks were referred to as "long-haired ones" (in reality they shaved their heads). This practice of avoiding taboo words shows that separation of Shinto and Buddhism remained the practice at the Ise Shrine, although there were movements to amalgamate the deities of Ise with Buddhas and Bodhisattvas.

Basho spent the summer of 1690 in a simple hut near Lake Biwa. There he wrote: "An ancient shrine is near, which so purifies my senses that I feel cleansed of the dust of the world"[18]—a timeless sentiment.

## The Development of Popular Ethics

In times of peace, learning prospers; not only the scholars retained by feudal lords but also townspeople developed their own ethical teachings. It was quite common for merchants, for example, to devote their spare time to scholarship, which was marked by a spirit of rationalism. One of these merchant-philosophers, Ishida Baigan (1685–1744), sought to elevate morality among ordinary men and women. He founded the **Shingaku** (Mind Learning) school, which preached in simple language "how to live the life of a sage." Adopting whatever he found expedient and good from Buddhism, Confucianism, and Shinto, Baigan developed a practical moral philosophy, which emphasized frugality, honesty, and forbearance as the virtues to be practiced. He taught that everyone was able to attain some degree of spiritual equilibrium regardless of his or her social class. He also affirmed commerce and profit-making as being in agreement with the way of heaven.[19]

## The Status of Women

Neo-Confucian morality, in accentuating the different functions of sexes, accorded girls and women a subservient place in society. Although the phrase "danson johi" (respect the male, denigrate the female) may be the creation of a later date, the idea was clearly put into practice during the Edo period. Certainly, the plight of women differed depending on their social class, their economic standing, and their individual circumstances; but generally speaking, women's social and spiritual status suffered severely. Wives of the samurai class were bound by the obligation of bearing sons, as only male children, and usually the first-born, were entitled to succeed the family line. No male child meant the abolition of the family, and for the feudal lords this meant the confiscation by the shogunate of their domains and their people. In order not to take any chances, feudal lords openly kept concubines, diminishing their wives to little more than childbearing tools.

A Neo-Confucian scholar, Kaibara Ekiken (1630–1714), brought the moral message of self-cultivation in simple language to all classes of people, especially women and children.[20] A popular booklet, the *Onna Daigaku* or *Greater Learning for Women*, attributed to him, was widely circulated after 1710. Culled by an anonymous author from the relevant passages of the writings of Ekiken, the booklet taught girls the virtues of "obedience" as their lifelong duty. A girl must practice filial piety toward her father and mother until her marriage, and after marriage she must honor her father-in-law and mother-in-law; for a married woman, her husband is her "lord" and she "must serve him with all worship and reverence." Listed as "five ills that afflict women" are "indocility," "discontent," "slander," "jealousy," and "silliness." A woman could be "returned" to her parents' home if found guilty of any of the "seven reasons for divorce," which include disobedience to her father-in-law or mother-in-law, failure to bear children, lewdness, jealousy, and foul diseases such as leprosy; the humiliation of divorce was to be initiated by her husband's family only.[21]

However, it would appear that there were some ways of escaping an oppressive marriage. The Tokeiji temple in Kamakura and the Mantokuji temple in the present-day Gunma Prefecture were two Buddhist nunneries where unhappily married women could "run to" to take refuge.[22] These temples acted as a sort of divorce court, and under their "jurisdiction," husbands were required to issue the paperwork that consented to divorce.

In a prevailing climate where the status of women was being increasingly undermined, the message of universal salvation offered by Kamakura Buddhist leaders (see Chapter 4) became overshadowed, and misogynistic ideas crept back into Buddhist practice. A salient example of this is the adoption of a Chinese apocryphal *sutra*, *Ketsubon-kyo* ("Blood Pond Hell Sutra"), which was used by some Buddhist temples to advocate the view that women contaminated the soil and the water by the blood of childbirth and of menstruation, and therefore they were destined to hell, unless proper rituals were performed by Buddhist priests.[23] It was partly in reaction to this kind of irrational oppression of women that popular religious movements arose in the late eighteenth and the early nineteenth centuries (see Chapter 7). Various taboos associated with menstruation, practiced in certain regions of Japan, were lifted only in 1872 by the decree of the Meiji government.

## The Discovery of Native Learning (Kokugaku)

Studies of classical Japanese literature, such as the **Kokin** poetry collection, *The Tale of Ise*, and *The Tale of Genji*, had been kept alive over the centuries by courtiers. During the eighteenth century, these studies became the vehicle for a renewal of the ancient Japanese religious-cultural heritage—a movement known as "Native Learning" (**Kokugaku**). The scholarly approach of those Neo-Confucians who returned to Confucius and Mencius seems in part to have prompted this discovery of the ancient ethical-cultural roots of the Japanese.

This *Kokugaku* movement got started with Kada Azumaro (1669–1736), the head priest of the Fushimi Inari Shrine in Kyoto, who made an extensive study of classical Japanese literature and came to the conclusion that a school dedicated to the study of ancient Japanese literature should be established. Azumaro's disciple, Kamo Mabuchi (1697–1769), found in the **Man'yo-shu** (an eighth-century compilation of Japanese poetry) the ethos of "masuraoburi" (masculinity, candor, and honesty), and praised it as the original Japanese sensibility. Mabuchi's disciple, Motoori Norinaga (1730–1801) took on the project of decoding the *Records of Ancient Matters* (*Kojiki*), which occupied him for thirty years. Through his study, Norinaga came to believe that this work preserved the original pure Japanese spirituality, free of Confucian and Buddhist influences. He also made a meticulous study of *The Tale of Genji*, and identified its prevailing feeling of "mono no aware"—gentle pathos and emotive empathy—as the pristine native Japanese sensibility.[24] Norinaga embraced the view that "the Japanese and their Shinto, when purged of all foreign accretions and influences, represented the pure, and therefore the best, inheritance of humanity from the divine ages."[25]

## "Hirata Shinto"

Hirata Atsutane (1776–1843), who became Norinaga's posthumous disciple, formulated his Shinto theology with a biblical interpretation. Writings by Jesuit missionaries were available even under the Tokugawa regime, in the form of Chinese translations imported from China. Having read the *Records of Ancient Matters*, Atsutane came to identify the first-mentioned deity, Ame-no-minaka-nushi ("Master of the August Center of Heaven") as none other than God the Creator. He discussed the importance of life after death, maintaining that good souls would ascend into Heaven, while bad ones would descend into the realm of eternal torment.[26] He asserted the uniqueness of Japan as the country divinely begotten by gods, "as a special mark of favor from the heavenly gods." Atsutane's argument went as follows: "Gods formed all the lands of the world at the Creation, and these gods were without exception born in Japan. Japan is thus the homeland of the gods, and that is why we call it the Land of the Gods."[27]

Atsutane's vigorous, though simplistic, Japano-centric teachings attracted quite a few followers; by the time his adopted son Kanetane was preaching, these numbered more than 3,700. The "nativist" argument invariably upheld that Japan's ancient native ethico-religious heritage was superior to foreign religious traditions. The ancient Japanese cultural roots, as found in "pure" (i.e. ancient) Shinto, became the source of Japanese self-identity. The ideology of a "return to antiquity" (*fukko*) became one of the main driving forces of the "pro-emperor, anti-foreigner" campaign which eventually toppled the Tokugawa shogunate.[28] It also laid the foundation for the making of Shinto into a national faith in the Meiji period (1868–1912) and beyond.

## Living Buddhism

Buddhism may have become a semi-official established religion, but its spiritual vitality was maintained by those who continued to inject life into the tradition and kept it a living faith. Suzuki Shozan (1579–1655), a samurai and Soto Zen priest, advocated Zen practice for all classes of people and attempted, though unsuccessfully, to persuade the shogunate to adopt Zen as the official religion. Two Rinzai masters, Bankei Eitaku (1622–1693) and Hakuin Ekaku (1685–1768), preached to ordinary men and women in a simple language; Hakuin, who systematized the *koan* practice and made it accessible to any aspirant, is especially credited with having revived the Rinzai tradition.

Jiun Onko (1718–1804), a Shingon Buddhist priest and accomplished Sanskrit scholar, revived the Vinaya (precepts) practice. At an advanced age, he established a Shinto sect which affirmed both Shinto and Buddhism as independent religions.

There had always been a stream of anonymous devout followers of the True Pure Land sect, who led spiritual lives of utmost humility, sincerity, and gratitude, for the saving grace of Amida Buddha. Their simple but powerful spiritual presence gained them the name "Myokonin" (marvelously blessed people).

Still other Buddhists found their spiritual freedom in an apolitical world, outside the confines of society. Ryokan (1758–1831), a Soto monk, calligrapher, and poet, adopted a simple lifestyle, free of possessions, while caring for the general well-being of other people.

*Sengai's drawing of a frog beneath a banana tree, with accompanying haiku verse, captures the more lighthearted side of Zen spirituality.*

Sengai (1750–1837), a Rinzai priest, calligrapher, and poet, lived in freedom afforded by his enlightenment (*satori*). He once made an ink drawing of a banana tree (basho) with a frog under it, to which he added a verse alluding to the poet Basho. One of the most celebrated *haiku* by Basho is the one about a frog jumping into the water: "Furuikeya kawazu tobikomu mizu no oto" ("Oh, ancient pond! The frog jumps in, 'Plop!'"). Sengai's haiku reads: "Ike araba tonde Basho ni kikasetai" ("Should there be a pond, I would jump in; I want Basho to hear my 'plop!'").[29] The subject of Sengai's poem and the drawing is a small frog, which looks at the world of humans from its own perspective. In Zen Buddhism, all sentient and non-sentient beings partake of the buddha nature. Sengai's humorous verse is a jewel of the Edo-period Zen culture, which combined Zen awareness with a lighthearted attitude toward the world, sustained by compassion for all beings.

## The Emergence of Popular Religious Movements

By the early years of the nineteenth century, the Tokugawa shogunate had begun to show signs of weakening, largely due to the failure of its economic policies. The lower echelons of samurai were now impoverished, while powerful merchants amassed large fortunes. Poor harvests  and high taxes contributed to the oppression of peasants. Partly in reaction to the social disorder, and partly in response to the loosening grip of the shogunate, popular religious movements sprang up at this time.

New sects formed around individuals who had unique religious experiences. They included the Tenri sect, founded in 1838 by a woman, Nakayama Miki (1798–1887); the Kurozumi sect, founded in 1814 by a man, Kurozumi Munetada (1780–1850); and the Konko sect, founded in 1859 by a man, Kawate Bunjiro or "Konko Daijin" (1814–90). Their doctrines were eclectic, taking elements from Buddhism, worship of Shinto deities, *yin–yang* cosmology, and other folk practices and beliefs. The common thread of these new religious sects was the founders' shamanic experience of possession. They were excellent healers; and their message of a positive outlook on life and a life of gratitude brought happiness and improved fortune to many of their followers. The Kurozumi sect emphasized the benevolent healing energy of the sun, and the goddess Amaterasu. These new religious sects upheld the equality of sexes— a sensibility deeply rooted in Japanese folk traditions, and a marked feature of the ancient Shinto worldview in which women, and more specifically their spiritual power, played an indispensable role.[1] These sects survive to this day. Followers of the Tenri sect established their own town of Tenri, south of Nara, and today they have nearly

*A nineteenth-century print showing pilgrim travelers carrying a portable shrine. Pilgrimages became increasingly popular from the fifteenth century; during the Edo period there were several massive pilgrimages to Ise, known as* okagemairi.

2 million followers. Both the Konko and the Kurozumi sects also have many adherents, 433,000 and 290,000 respectively.

A periodic nationwide pilgrimage to Ise, known as ***okagemairi*** (literally, thanksgiving visit), had taken place in 1650, 1705, 1718, and 1771, but the last and largest one was the 1830 *okagemairi*, which lasted for five months and involved one in every six or seven Japanese men and women (and children). The visit to the Ise Shrine had become a hugely popular tradition, and even the shogunate had no choice but to allow these pilgrimages to take place. Apart from the *okagemairi*, the individual pilgrimage to Ise, known as the "**Ise *mairi*,**" had been popular since the fifteenth century. Because the travel expenses to Ise from distant places were considerable, villagers established a communal savings account, and whenever this contained ample funds, one or two representatives went on the pilgrimage on behalf of all the villagers.

The symbol of Japan *par excellence*, Mt. Fuji, also became a pilgrimage site for the followers of the Fuji sect, which had been established in the eighteenth century. This sect was known for its radically egalitarian view of the sexes. Women, traditionally forbidden to climb sacred mountains, were allowed to participate in the pilgrimages of 1800 and 1860.[2] Although the number of followers is dwindling, the Fuji sect and other related sects survive to this day.

## The Opening of the Ports and the Resurfacing of the "Hidden Christians"

In the nineteenth century, foreign ships began to arrive in Japan, pressuring the shogunate to abandon its policy of port closure. In 1858, the shogunate signed a commercial treaty with the United States; and soon thereafter it reached similar agreements with Russia, France, Britain, and the Netherlands. The following year, several French Catholic priests, a Russian Orthodox priest, and several American Protestant missionaries of various denominations arrived in Japan as chaplains to their respective consulates, or in some related capacity. The adoption of Christianity by Japanese people was still prohibited by the shogunate, however, and the missionaries (who were proficient in the Japanese language) had to carry out their work surreptitiously. They began their work at the port towns of Nagasaki, Yokohama, and Hakodate, where communities of foreign tradesmen were established.

From the beginning, the French Catholics worked with impoverished peasants to improve their lives. American Protestant missionaries mainly targeted young intellectual men of the samurai class. The Russian Orthodox priest Nicolai was especially successful with a group of young samurai in Hakodate.

French Catholic priests in Nagasaki were hopeful that they might find the descendants of the Japanese Christians who had been converted before the prohibition of Christianity—and so they did. On March 17, 1865, fourteen or fifteen villagers from Urakami visited the cathedral just erected in Nagasaki. To Father Bernard Petitjean's astonished delight, one of them approached him and said: "We are of the same mind as you; where is the holy statue of Santa Maria?"[3] The Japanese Christians who had been in hiding (*kakure kirishitan*) resurfaced on that day.

## The Meiji Restoration

An anti-shogunate movement gained momentum during the 1850s, and in the following decade the royalist samurai gathered in Kyoto to promote their cause. The slogan "Revere the emperor, expel the foreigners," began to be heard everywhere. Becoming ambitious, the emperor Komei (r. 1846–66) hoped to recover the throne's long-lost political power. However, he died of a mysterious ailment in 1866 (rumor had it that he was poisoned), and Mutsuhito (the future Emperor Meiji), then only in his teens, was enthroned. In 1867, mass frenzy swept through the entire country. Mobs attacked the mansions of local mayors and wealthy merchants, and went on a rampage of looting and carousing. The Tokugawa shogunate's rule came to a standstill; the last shogun, Yoshinobu, resigned in October 1867; and political power was transferred to the imperial court with the arrival of the New Year, 1868. This power-transfer from the shogun to the emperor is known as the Meiji Restoration. Once the new government had taken control, the mass hysteria subsided. The government established its administrative seat in Edo—which was renamed Tokyo, the "eastern capital," in July—and adopted the new era name of "Meiji" in September. The emperor briefly visited Edo in 1868, and returned permanently the following March, settling in the Imperial Palace—the former Edo Castle.

The emperor was a figurehead, however, and the actual power of the new Meiji government was in the hands of the upper echelon of government officials, made up of court nobles and meritorious samurai who had sided with the imperial court and who successfully brought about the transition of power from the shogun to the emperor. From the beginning, the new government was Janus-faced. It looked to the West in adopting progressive policies in order to "encourage industry, strengthen the economy, and build up a strong army," but it also looked to Japan's ancient religious and cultural roots, which fostered a nationalistic and conservative agenda. These two contradictory directions—the creation of a modern industrial and capitalist nation-state while returning to the country's ancient roots—eventually coalesced in State Shinto (*Kokka Shinto*), the state-sponsored Shinto shrine system.

## The Separation of Shinto and Buddhism

Among the policymakers of the early Meiji government were students of the Hirata school of Shinto and followers of "Native Learning" (*Kokugaku*), who aspired to resurrect the ancient theocratic polity.[4] In March 1868, the Meiji government declared its intent to "unite the church and the state" and issued a decree separating Shinto from Buddhism (*shinbutsu bunri-rei*), which aimed at elevating the status of Shinto above Buddhism. On a doctrinal level, this meant that the "essence-manifestation" theory which had amalgamated Shinto and Buddhism for centuries had to be dissolved. This caused much confusion, because many Shinto deities now had Buddhist titles, such as "Gongen" (Buddha's avatar) and "Bosatsu" (Bodhisattva). Besides, many Shinto shrines housed Buddhist statues, which now had to be moved to nearby Buddhist temples.

This edict of the "separation of Shinto and Buddhism" triggered a frenzy of anti-Buddhist violence in many parts of Japan. The first shrine to be attacked was the Hie (or Hiyoshi) Shrine, which was the epitome of Buddhist–Shinto syncretism as the protector of Enryakuji at Mt. Hiei. Shinto clerics and crowds attacked various buildings on the Hie Shrine compound, destroying precious Buddhist statues and images. This wave of destruction spread swiftly to other parts of the country. In response to a petition from the powerful Honganji and other Buddhist temples, the government issued a communication stating that the "separation" did not mean the "destruction" of Buddhism. The attacks on Buddhist temples subsided within a year or two, although lingering hostilities persisted for several more years.[5]

## The Image of the Emperor as a *Kami*

In the early years of Meiji, ordinary Japanese people, accustomed to a shogun, had only a vague idea of an emperor. There was even a rumor that the "Son of Heaven" (another title for the emperor) was in fact an incarnation of a mythical dragon creature and that in his trail one would find scales! The quickest way to educate the masses that the emperor existed was to resurrect the association between the emperor and the sun goddess, Amaterasu.[6] Thus, the ancient concept of the sacred emperor as a living *kami* was revived.

In 1872, the government issued "Three principles," commanding all the Japanese to (1) "respect the *kami* deities and love the country," (2) "observe the way of heaven and practice the way of humanity," and (3) "serve the emperor and respect the will of the imperial court." The government called Shinto priests as well as Buddhist monks and nuns to "educate" the Japanese, and to this end set up the Office of the Great Teaching (*Daikyoin*). In response, Mori Arinori (1847–89), a diplomat stationed in the United States, and Shimaji Mokurai (1838–1911), a True Pure Land priest touring Europe, each protested against this policy of imposing a pseudo-religion on the Japanese people. Besides, the uneasy alliance of Buddhists and Shintoists was doomed to fail, and the Office of the Great Teaching was abolished in 1875. The government's initial attempt to institute a state religion had failed.

## Abolition of Old Festivals, New Festivals Created

One way in which the Meiji government set out to eradicate the Tokugawa legacy was to abolish the lunar calendar and adopt the Western-style Gregorian calendar. This took effect from January 1, 1873. The government also abolished the traditional five "seasonal festivities" (*sekku*), and in their stead instituted new state-approved holidays, such as the Day of the Founding of the Nation (February 11), the Birthday of the Meiji Emperor (November 3), and the Harvest Day (November 23). However, some well-loved traditional festivals, such as the peach blossom celebration ("Girls' Day," March 3), and the "Star Festival" (July 7), survived this official weeding.

In its effort to modernize Japan the government lifted many ancient taboos. Most sacred mountains became accessible to women, and Buddhist monks and foreigners were allowed to enter the inner sanctuary of the Ise Shrine. The government also considered many forms of folk religious practices to be "old-fashioned" and banned such customs as the worship of the "protector deity of the boundaries" (*dosojin*), the *nenbutsu*-dance, and the festival of the Bodhisattva **Jizo** (protector of children). Many of these religious icons and festivals are today practically forgotten. The government also prohibited the activities of mediums and shamans. In this process of standardization, rich local religious customs and rituals began to disappear one by one.

## Lifting the Ban on Christianity

The prohibition of Christianity continued beyond the fall of the Tokugawa shogunate in 1867. In 1868, Kido Takayoshi, a high official of the new government, was dispatched to the predominantly Christian village of Urakami to deliver its policy on Christianity. This stated that since the Japanese were descendants of the goddess Amaterasu, they ought to worship the emperor, who was the parent-figure, and that it was wrong to embrace a foreign religion, because the true intention of the Catholic priests was to take over Japan.[7] Remarkably, all 3,000 Christian villagers stuck to their faith and accepted the punishment of exile to various parts of Japan. In exile, more than 600 died of torture or poor living conditions, and over 1,000 apostatized.

At around this time, in late 1871, a delegation of eminent government ministers, headed by Iwakura Tomomi, set out on a two-year tour of the United States and Europe. The purpose of this "Iwakura Mission" was to study the institutions of the Western nations, with a view to adopting those suited to Japan and so raise the country's status in the world. The delegates saw first-hand the importance of Christianity in the countries they visited, which made them realize how embarrassing was the news from home of the persecution of the Urakami Christians. They telegraphed Tokyo to stop the persecution.[8] The Japanese ban against Christianity was lifted in February 1873, while the Iwakura Mission was still abroad. Survivors among the exiled Christians of Urakami triumphantly returned to their home village, and those who had renounced their faith repented their deed and were allowed to convert back to Catholicism.

## The Invention of State Shinto

After the failed attempt to institute Shinto as the state religion, the government adopted a more subtle approach. They artificially separated "religious practices" (especially those practices that were features of the "mountain cult sects," including the offshoots of the Fuji sect) and "rituals" (such as visiting shrines and bowing in front of the main altar), removing the former and retaining the latter. During the 1880s, Shinto sects that were considered religious were granted independent sectarian status and classified under the "sect Shinto." On the surface it looked as though these sects finally had the government's approval, but the truth was that they were considered hindrances to creating a "national rite," which should be purely ritualistic. In order to designate this national rite, the government adopted the word "**Jinja**" (Shinto shrine) instead of "Shinto," and insisted that the rituals associated with the Jinja "are not religion (*shukyo*) but a national rite (*saishi*)."[9]

## The Meiji Constitution and the Imperial Rescript on Education

The divinity of the emperor was woven into the Meiji Constitution of 1889. Article One reads: "The Empire of Japan shall be reigned over and governed by a line of Emperors unbroken for ages eternal," and Article Three reads: "The Emperor is sacred and inviolable." Freedom of religion was set forth in Article Twenty-eight: "The subjects shall, within limits not prejudicial to peace and order, and not antagonistic to their duties as subjects, enjoy freedom of religious belief." This qualified "freedom of religion" left ample room for the government to prosecute, in later days, those who did not obey the government's measures of thought control, and to charge them with the crime of *lèse-majesté*, a transgression against the inviolable divine emperor.

In the following year, the government issued the ***Imperial Rescript on Education***, whose purpose was to implant in the minds of Japanese children the image of the emperor as sacred and as the "father" figure to the Japanese people.[10] A copy of the rescript was distributed to every school in the country and enshrined in a sacred altar specifically built for it. Every student was taught to pay the utmost reverence to it.

This *Imperial Rescript on Education* immediately came into conflict with Christianity in the person of a schoolteacher, Uchimura Kanzo (1861–1930). In January 1891, at the ceremony of the elite First Higher School in Tokyo, Uchimura refused to bow in front of a copy of the Rescript. The press picked up on this incident and sensationalized it, triggering a nationwide debate as to whether Christianity was compatible with Japanese education. Although Uchimura was forced to resign from his teaching position, leading Christians, such as Uemura Masahisa (1857–1912) and Ebina Danjo (1856–1937), defended the Christian faith. In the end the "Uchimura incident" had the effect of strengthening Japanese Christianity. In 1899, the government issued a decree that officially legalized Christianity. In 1912, the home minister organized a conference of "three religions"—Buddhism, Shinto, and Christianity—and made them pledge their loyalty to the state. In this way, Christianity, though officially recognized, was at the same time incorporated into the emperor-centered political system, and effectually subjugated to the national rite centered in the worship at Shinto shrines.

## Christianity in Modern Japan

Yamaji Aizan (1864–1917), a social critic, made an often-quoted observation that the sons of the former samurai class that sided with the shogunate at the time of the Meiji Restoration—and the shogunate turned out to be the "wrong side"—tended to convert to Christianity because they saw little chance of success in the new government.[11] Indeed, many influential Japanese Christians, such as Uemura Masahisa and Uchimura Kanzo, were born into high-ranking samurai families. For them, the attraction of Christianity was largely its message of the dignity of the individual and inviolable human rights in the sight of God, along with its universal orientation. Uemura did much to make Christianity Japanese; he was among the team of learned Christians who translated the Bible into Japanese; he also founded, in Tokyo, a Protestant seminary which trained younger generations of Japanese pastors. Uchimura Kanzo advocated Christian spirituality, free from the constraints of an organized Church. Many Japanese Christians of the Meiji period studied in Europe and the United States and became spokesmen for Western humanism and democracy, which added to the attraction of Christianity among the socially concerned.

Catholicism made headway among underprivileged people, as priests and nuns concentrated on social work as an effective means to win converts. They built hospitals and orphanages, and introduced innovative agricultural and dairy farming practices. At the same time Catholicism also penetrated upper-class Japanese society, as the Catholic missions established many reputable schools, which excelled especially in advancing the education of women and children.

Although Christianity never fully took root in Japan, and today Japanese Christians (Protestants and Catholics combined) account for just about 1 percent of the entire population, the impact of Christianity on modern Japan has been far from negligible. This is because many leading intellectuals and educators have been Christians. For instance, Niijima Jo (1843–90), who smuggled himself out of Japan in 1864 to study in the United States, was baptized into the Protestant faith; and in 1875, a year after his return to Japan, he established the Doshisha (now Doshisha University) in Kyoto. Christian teachings of universal love and the virtues of charity, humility, and selflessness have inspired a small but often influential group of Japanese. Among them was the scholar of political science, Nanbara Shigeru (1889–1974), who became a Christian under the influence of Ebina Danjo and Uchimura Kanzo. In the post-World War II period, Nanbara became the president of Tokyo University and led the move toward educational reform.

## Spiritual Movements Among Leading Intellectuals

The separation of Shinto and Buddhism occasioned some self-reflection among concerned Buddhists. A government communication of 1872, which "allowed" Buddhist clerics "to eat meat, marry, and let their hair grow," fundamentally threatened the integrity of Buddhist precepts. To meet this challenge, such leaders as the Pure Land priest Fukuda Gyokai (1806–88), the Shingon priest Shaku Unsho (1827–1909), and Ouchi Seiran (1845–1918), a former Soto Zen monk who became a social activist, launched a movement to promote authentic Buddhist practice. As part of their effort, they especially encouraged the practice of Buddhism among laymen.

It is a hallmark of the Meiji intellectual world that many of its leading thinkers engaged in a spiritual quest. This possibly reflected the rapidly changing society of the time, in which traditional self-identity was disappearing. A university-trained columnist and member of the elite, Takayama Chogyu (1871–1902), caused a sensation when he converted to the Nichiren sect. In 1914, Tanaka Chigaku (1861–1939), disappointed with the Nichiren sect, established the Kokuchukai, a lay organization which aimed to go back to the true spirit of Nichiren himself.

Kiyozawa Manshi (1863–1903), a True Pure Land priest who trained in Western philosophy under Ernest F. Fenollosa (1852–1908) at the Imperial University in Tokyo, took up strict observance of Buddhist precepts, reminiscent of an early Indian Buddhist monk. His intense spiritual life attracted like-minded followers, and in 1901 the group began publishing a journal, called *Seishinkai* ("The Spiritual World"), which exerted considerable influence upon the younger generation of the day. Tsunashima Ryosen (1873–1907) subjected his spiritual experiences to an ethical–anthropological scrutiny; his account of a mystical experience drew the attention of those engaged in a spiritual quest. Nishida Tenko (1872–1968), who was aiming for an ideal and just society, came to the realization that "spiritual innocence" was the primary mode of being; in 1905 he established Ittoen, a community of seekers in Kyoto, which thrives to this day.

Many intellectuals of the Meiji period were drawn to Zen Buddhism. The celebrated novelist Natsume Soseki (1867–1916) was interested in Zen practice, although he did not formally take it up. Suzuki Teitaro (better known as Daisetz T. Suzuki; 1870–1966), trained under Zen Master Shaku Soen (1859–1919) of Engakuji, in Kamakura, published widely in both Japanese and English; today he is known as the pioneer who introduced Zen Buddhism into the West. Shaku Soen, who represented the Japanese Zen tradition at the 1893 World Parliament of Religions in Chicago, traveled to the United States twice, and accepted Americans among his students. A philosopher, Nishida Kitaro (1870–1945)—D. T. Suzuki's lifelong friend—also undertook Zen practice, which led him to create his philosophical vision of the "unity" of opposites—such as space and time, spirit and matter, self-consciousness and objective consciousness, and the individual and the world. A writer, Kurata Hyakuzo (1891–1943), represented the younger generation of spiritual seekers, and his writings influenced the students of the Taisho period (1912–26).

An account of Meiji spirituality cannot ignore the unique contribution of Hiratsuka Raicho (1886–1971), the "mother" of the Japanese women's movement. She was an adept practitioner of Zen; her awakening was authenticated by two Zen masters on separate occasions. Hiratsuka drew her energy and her egalitarian outlook on life from her Zen experience. She organized a literary group among socially conscious young women, and they began the publication of a journal, *Seito* ("Bluestockings") in 1911. In an essay that opened the inaugural volume of this journal, Hiratsuka declared: "In antiquity, we women were the brilliant sun." She was a social activist all her life, supporting movements against nuclear weapons and participating in an anti-Vietnam War demonstration. Her indomitable spirit was a fine example of the power of a woman's spirituality, which resonated with ancient native memory, combined with a formal religious discipline and spiritual awakening.

## Scholarship and the Buddhist Faith

During the Meiji period, objective studies of religions flourished as Japanese scholars adopted Western methods of scholarship. Through the work of scholars such as Anesaki Masaharu (1873–1949), who established the discipline of religious studies at Tokyo Imperial University, original Buddhist practices received much attention; this led to the religious movement of "back to original Buddhism," which added a new dimension to Japanese religious experience. The project of compiling and publishing Buddhist scriptures in Chinese began in 1924; called the *Taisho Shinshu Daizokyo*, this collection is an indispensable source for scholars of Buddhism.

## The Establishment of Omoto

A new Shinto-based sect, Omoto, was established in 1899 by a healer-shaman, Deguchi Nao (1837–1918), and her son-in-law Deguchi Onizaburo (1871–1948). They were often possessed by *kami* spirits and were excellent healers. Onizaburo deliberately took Susanoo (the younger brother of the sun goddess) as the main deity of their sect, which was a clear break from the state-sponsored cult of

Amaterasu and the imperial family. He was a prolific writer and a charismatic spiritual figure, and under his leadership the sect grew into a considerable presence. Followers were taught by Onizaburo to develop their spiritual faculty, through which they could commune with cosmic spiritual forces. Onizaburo also promoted organic farming and creative activities, such as pottery—all a means of communing with the universal energy. Because the sect was critical of the government's religious policy, it was persecuted three times, but each time it survived and expanded. At the same time it spawned yet more new sects, including Seicho no Ie (1930) and Sekai Kyu-seikyo (1935), which in turn produced the Mahikari sect.

## From the Taisho to the Showa Period

During the Taisho period, democratic and socialist movements flourished, and Marxist ideology began to spread among intellectuals. However, the government came to fear that such social and intellectual movements would undermine the political form whose foundation rested on the idea of the divine emperor—a political form called the "emperor system" (*ten'no-sei*), or the "national polity" or "national essence" (*kokutai*). In 1925, the government issued the peace ordinance, effectively a form of legislation to enforce thought control. Over the following decade, the government aggressively cracked down on socialism, Marxism, and even Western liberalism, regarding them as counter to the "emperor-system."

In December 1926, upon the death of the emperor Taisho, Crown Prince Hirohito succeeded to the throne. This was a turbulent time: the Japanese economy had since 1924 been plummeting to an all-time low, partly due to post-World War I inflation and exacerbated by the expensive damage caused by the Kanto earthquake of 1923, which devastated the Tokyo–Yokohama area. In the spring of 1927, following a careless remark made by the finance minister, people flocked to banks to withdraw their savings, forcing small and midsize banks into bankruptcy. This financial chaos had a destabilizing effect on the lives of the people. The birth of new religious groups at this time, many of them based on the teachings of Nichiren, was no doubt connected to a general yearning for peace of mind and spiritual comfort. A lay Buddhist sect, Reiyukai, established in 1924 by Kubo Kakutaro (1892–1944) and his sister-in-law Kotani Kimi (1901–71), emphasized the importance of proper care of ancestral spirits. The founders were endowed with shamanic ability and the power of healing, and Reiyukai gained a large number of followers. Another sect, Soka Gakkai, was established in 1930 by two educators, Makiguchi Tsunesaburo (1871–1944) and Toda Josei (1900–56), who held that the purpose of life consists in the pursuit of happiness, which is achieved by transforming oneself in accordance with the value system of beauty, benefit, and good (as opposed to ugliness, harm, and evil), based on Buddhism, as expounded by Nichiren. Because of their uncompromising anti-government attitude, both Makiguchi and Toda were imprisoned in 1943, and Makiguchi died in prison in 1944. Meanwhile, in 1938, Naganuma Myoko (1889–1957) and Niwano Nikkyo (1906–99) broke away from Reiyukai and established a new sect, Rissho Koseikai, which upheld the primary importance of the teachings of the *Lotus Sutra*. Another new sect, Hitonomichi Kyodan, was established 1925 by Miki Tokuharu (1871–1938), whose doctrine was based primarily on the tradition of mountain asceticism. This sect was persecuted by the government and disbanded in 1937, only to reorganize itself in 1946 under the leadership of the founder's son, Miki Tokuchika (1900–83), as Perfect Liberty Kyodan.

## The Implementation of State Shinto

According to imperial family tradition, a newly enthroned emperor is obliged to undergo a formal enthronement ceremony, and this Emperor Hirohito did in November 1928. The following year happened to be the year of the fifty-eighth *sengu* of the Ise Shrine (see Chapter 2). Resplendent imperial ceremonies and ancient Shinto rituals delighted the people, who had been living in the shadow of economic and social depression. It was a time when they were disposed to embrace Shinto. Teachers took children and students to local Shinto shrines to worship as part of school activities. "Shrine Shinto" as the national rite was thus gradually taking shape. In 1930, this practice elicited reactions from the True Pure Land sect and from the Japanese Christians' Association; their respective doctrines forbade their followers to worship the *kami* deities.

Whether or not the rituals at Shinto shrines were religious acts became an urgent question in April 1932, when a handful of Catholic students at Sophia University, in Tokyo (founded by the Jesuits), refused to participate in the special ritual held at the Yasukuni Shrine (see below) to commemorate the recent war dead (possibly those who died in the 1931 unauthorized military machination, known as the "Manchurian Incident"). The Catholic Church issued a statement declaring that if the act of worship at the Shinto shrines was a religious act, Christian dogma forbade its followers to participate in it. The reply issued by the vice-minister of education read: "Worship at Shinto shrines does not constitute a religious act, but it is part of the school activities; it is the expression of one's patriotism. For this reason, personal religious conviction should not deter anyone from worshipping at Shinto shrines."[12] Henceforth, no Japanese student was exempted from worship at Shinto shrines.

## The Yasukuni Shrine

The Yasukuni Shrine grew out of the Shokonsha (literally, "shrine that beckons back the souls"), which had been erected in May 1868 in the Higashiyama district of Kyoto as the shrine to those who died fighting to achieve the Meiji Restoration. The following year it was moved to Tokyo, on the southwestern side of the imperial palace; ten years later, in 1879, it was renamed the Yasukuni Shrine—"Yasukuni" meaning "the peace of the country"—and made into the national mausoleum of fallen soldiers. It rose in status as Japan successfully fought a war with China in 1894–95 and with Russia in 1904–05. During the Russo–Japanese War, especially, it became necessary to impress on otherwise reluctant soldiers the glory of fighting and dying for country and emperor. Honoring the war dead at this national shrine was one way of cultivating a spirit of self-sacrifice and military patriotism; it also justified, perversely, the imperialistic war effort by enshrining the fallen soldiers' souls.

## The War Effort and State Shinto

By the mid-1930s Japan was turning into a totalitarian society, and fanatical ultranationalistic forces began to prevail. By 1940 the Japanese government was in the hands of military officers, who promoted an expansionist policy in Asia. Those ultranationalists found justification for their action in the words of the legendary Emperor Jinmu, who had declared that the establishment of a capital of Japan would "unite all corners of the land under one roof" (*hakko iu*)—a passage from the *Chronicles of Japan* (*Nihongi*).[13] It was not that Japanese people did not recognize such reasoning to be anachronistic; rather, one could no longer voice criticism of the government, unless one were willing to risk a charge of *lèse-majesté*, imprisonment, and torture.

In 1940, the Office of Shinto Shrines (*Jinjakyoku*), which had been set up to promote State Shinto, was renamed the Shrine Board (*Jingi'in*), which virtually elevated State Shinto to the uncontested status of national faith. By the time Japan plunged into total war, in 1941, the flag of the sun (*hinomaru*) and the Ise Shrine had come to be associated with military victory, and the government adopted the word *kamikaze* (the "divine wind" that blows on the coast of Ise) for the squad of young pilots who were to carry out suicide missions. Thus, ancient, august symbols were appropriated to serve the new militarism.

## The Postwar Dismantling of State Shinto

Japanese military aggression ended with the catastrophe of Hiroshima and Nagasaki, where atomic bombs were dropped on August 6 and 9, 1945. Japan unconditionally surrendered to the Allied forces on August 15, 1945, bringing World War II to an end. The Allied Occupation forces organized the office of the Supreme Commander for the Allied Powers (SCAP), set up the Religious Division under the Civil Information and Education Section, and began dismantling State Shinto, which SCAP deemed to have been at the core of Japanese militarism and ultranationalism. In December 1945, the "Shinto Directive" was issued, ordering the separation of religion and state and guaranteeing the people freedom of faith.[14]

On New Year's Day of 1946, Emperor Hirohito issued the "Declaration of Humanity," which denied the "myth" that he was a living *kami*. One passage reads:

> The ties between us [the imperial family] and our people
> have always stood upon mutual trust and affection. They do
> not depend upon mere legends and myths. They are not
> predicated on the false conception that the emperor is divine
> (*akitsu kami*), and that the Japanese people are superior to
> other races and fated to rule the world.[15]

On February 2, 1946, SCAP abolished the Shrine Board, putting an end to State Shinto, which had effectively existed for eighty years.

## The Rise of More New Sects

The freedom of religion guaranteed by SCAP unleashed a host of popular religious movements; it is said that one religious sect was formed every seven days. This proliferation of new sects, dubbed "the rush hour of gods," continued into the 1950s.[16] By the end of 1951, the number of religious organizations registered at the Ministry of Education had reached 720.[17] Today, the number easily exceeds 3,000.[18]

In the upsurge of religious movements, prewar religious sects, such as Soka Gakkai, Reiyukai, Rissho Koseikai, and Perfect Liberty Kyodan, gained huge numbers of followers. The success of these religious organizations is largely attributable to the restructuring of the social fabric brought about by the rapid urbanization of the 1960s. With the move of people away from small villages to large cities, the traditional family and social matrix broke down, and city dwellers, cut off from their roots, sought emotional and spiritual comfort. For instance, the Rissho Koseikai sect, which features group counseling sessions (*hoza*), gained over 1 million members in 1954; today its membership exceeds 7.6 million. The Perfect Liberty Kyodan, which promotes self-improvement through artistic creativity,[19] today has more than 1.2 million members. Soka Gakkai became

*The abolition of State Shinto was a priority for the occupying Allied powers. Posters such as this announced the occupation policy of guaranteeing freedom of faith for all Japanese.*

not only a religious phenomenon but also a political power, with its own political party, "Komei"; its membership soared from three hundred thousand in 1954 to some 17 million in 1990.[20] By rough count, one in five Japanese belongs to one of these enormously popular religious sects.

Although the prewar state-sponsored shrine system was dismantled, some of its spirit manages to survive. In 1956, 80,000 Shinto shrines (out of some 110,000) organized a coalition, Jinja Honcho (Association of Shinto Shrines), with the Ise Shrine at the head.[21] The status of the Yasukuni Shrine, with its militaristic and ultranationalistic associations, has remained a source of controversy. From around 1955, there was a move to bring the Yasukuni Shrine under the government's patronage, and in 1969, the Yasukuni Shrine Bill was presented at the Diet (parliament). It met fierce opposition from most religious organizations, and the bill was rescinded.[22] The debate over the status of the Yasukuni Shrine, however, continues to this day.

| Japanese Religions in the New Millennium | 8 |
|---|---|

## "New-New" Religious Sects

The rapid economic development that took place in Japan in the 1960s and beyond was not made without the sacrifice of a rich, humanistic, cultural and spiritual tradition. Unlike the people of the Meiji period, most Japanese in the postwar period have been too busy to reflect on moral and religious questions. Meanwhile, society has became highly competitive and people's lives stress-ridden—a situation that has elicited the formation, since the late 1970s, of yet more new religious sects, including Suko Mahikari (1978), Agonshu (1981), and Aum Shinrikyo (1984). These "new-new religions," as they are sometimes called, share certain general characteristics. For one thing, their doctrines are highly eclectic, incorporating elements from various religious traditions and spiritual systems of the world, just like the new-age movements in the West. These new-new religions generally guarantee the followers some sort of mystical experience and healing. Their messages are aimed largely at individuals rather than at the family unit.[1]

### The Rise and Fall of Aum Shinrikyo

The Aum Shinrikyo sect, founded by Asahara Shoko in 1984, reveals a troubling aspect of religious cults. Exotic and mystical elements of Asahara's teaching appealed to isolated, lonely, aimless youngsters. Asahara opened up a new world of spiritual life and mysticism to them. Borrowing from Transcendental Meditation, Asahara, calling himself a "guru," claimed that adept followers gained the ability to levitate. He also promised followers mystical trips, which were induced by hallucinogenic drugs, an overdose of which killed a number of "initiates." Under Asahara's manoeuvering, misguided followers became "robots" whose function was to bring about their teacher's prophecy of the end of the world. Still fresh in the memory today is the atrocity committed by certain members of Aum Shinrikyo, who in March 1995 killed twelve people and injured more than five thousand in a gas attack on the Tokyo subway. With the arrest of the culprits, criminal malpractices of the sect were unearthed, and subsequently most followers left. On January 18, 2000, Aum Shinrikyo reemerged with a new name, "Aleph," the first letter of the Hebrew alphabet, which means "infinity." Today, the sect has some eight hundred followers.

Statements by former members of Aum Shinrikyo testify that they were looking for a way to better the world, or to affirm their spirituality, or that they simply sought a community of like-minded idealists.[2] These innocent needs were subverted by the founder. Placing the Aum incident in the context of Japan's modern history, the historian and critic R. J. Lifton has argued that Japanese society's experience of two radical transformations—the Meiji Restoration and the defeat in World War II—caused deep trauma in the national psyche, and that this "psychohistorical dislocation" underlies the Aum incident.[3]

## The Religious Phenomenon of *Mizuko Kuyo*

Somewhere in the mid-1970s, a new religious phenomenon of offering Buddhist memorial services (**kuyo**) for unborn fetuses and stillborn babies, known as "mizuko kuyo," became popular. "Mizuko" literally means "water-child." It is said that about two-thirds of Japanese women have to resort to abortion to practice family planning, mainly for financial reasons because children's education is very expensive in today's Japan. Certainly, abortion is not a light matter and can leave psychological scars on young mothers. Many of these women turn to Buddhist temples to have memorial services performed. Such ceremonies seem to originate from the feeling of anxiety or guilt on the part of these women, but some scholars argue that they are prompted by fear of "revenge of an angry spirit" (*tatari*). Still others find feminist issues in the debate around abortion and *mizuko kuyo*, which they see as a social phenomenon that reflects a heavily male-dominated society.[4] No doubt, there is no one answer that explains *mizuko kuyo* in its totality. Be that as it may, the women perceive memorial services as a means of allowing the spirits of the unborn to rest in peace and of sending them off to heaven; in turn, they feel that their own sense of guilt is removed. Most women purchase from the temple a small stone statue of Bodhisattva Jizo, the protector of children, and place it on the temple ground, a practice analogous to erecting a gravestone. Often a knitted cap is placed on the head of the statue and a bib hung around its neck; these little extras express the mother's concern that a bare statue, somehow identified with the baby, would be cold without the cap and could not eat without the bib. *Mizuko kuyo* is performed not only in popular Buddhist temples but also by many Buddhism-based religious sects.

## Japanese Religions Today

If asked their religion, two out of three Japanese people today would answer that they have no personal religious faith. Two things may account for this. One is that religious activities have become cultural activities, so ingrained in the lives of the Japanese people that their religious origin is no longer recognized. This would explain the fact that on the first three days of the New Year, 2001, more than 88 million Japanese (about 70 percent of the population) crowded into Shinto shrines and Buddhist temples throughout the country to usher in the new millennium—but they consider this a non-religious act. The traditional year-end general cleaning, whose origin goes back to the Shinto proclivity for cleanliness, continues to be performed in most households; and these days, small cleaning businesses advertise their availability to do the job.

The other reason for the apparent lack of a need for religious affiliation is the fact that Buddhist temples have long been social institutions. Many families still belong to Buddhist temples—the legacy of the *danka* system (see Chapter 6)—but individual family members are not conscious of that formal affiliation on a day-to-day basis. Only at the time of a funeral do they discover it. Over 90 percent of Japanese funerals are conducted according to Buddhist rites.

Most of the Buddhist schools and sects of the past still thrive to this day; the monasteries at Mt. Hiei, Mt. Koya, and Eiheiji are still the major training centers of monks, and there are nunneries for female aspirants. The Aum Shinrikyo incident provoked much soul-searching among the more orthodox faiths; here was evidence that they were not meeting many of people's spiritual needs. Accordingly, some reforms were adopted. For example, the Japanese Association of Buddhism issued a statement in January 2000 that Buddhist temples would no longer charge for their service of conferring a

Buddhist name and a title (*kaimyo*) on the dead—a kind of "passport to paradise." Until then, bereaved families had been paying the priest about $2,000 as a token of thanks for the *kaimyo* conferred on the deceased. Japanese Buddhist institutions are now making an effort to bring themselves up to date and be socially meaningful.

Understandably, many Japanese still find Shinto intellectually repugnant because of its prewar association with the ultranationalistic State Shinto. But on the popular level, people flock to Shinto shrines to gain the protection of the *kami* deities; these worshippers include students facing entrance exams, single people looking for marriage partners, expectant mothers, people worried by illness in their family, merchants praying for good business, and fishermen and farmers praying for a good catch or a rich harvest. Where there are wishes, there will always be Shinto shrines for the Japanese.

## Looking Toward the Future

On August 9, 1999, conservative politicians, who held a majority in the Japanese Diet, voted to adopt the "rising sun" (*hinomaru*) as the official national flag and the song "Ours is Your Majesty's Reign" (*kimigayo*) as the national anthem, in preparation for Japan entering the new millennium. Before the passage of the bill, the government insisted that displaying the national flag and singing the anthem were "optional" at school ceremonies, but in 2001 the Ministry of Science and Education unilaterally adopted the position that they were mandatory. Also in 2001, domestic concerns were raised by the declared intention of newly elected prime minister Koizumi to worship as head of state at the Yasukuni Shrine, with all its imperial connotations, on August 15—the day that commemorates the end of World War II; this also elicited criticism from both the South Korean and the Chinese governments. In order to avoid international friction, the prime minister's advisors shifted forward the date of his visit to the shrine by two days.

The dramatic collapse of the Japanese economy in the early 1990s impacted on all sectors of the nation's life. In the wake of corporations' downsizing and restructuring, large numbers of workers lost their jobs. Many of these workers had devoted everything to their companies, for their entire life. Now, at a relatively advanced age, they found themselves with no sense of direction, which prompted them for the first time to question the meaning of their lives. Crushed by financial burden, a number of owners of small businesses committed suicide—a phenomenon that persists to this day. For other workers, religion, as the carrier of fundamental values or the source of spiritual healing, is once again becoming meaningful. In this atmosphere, established religions continue to adapt themselves to the new needs of the people, while many more "new" religions will no doubt arise.

Ecological crises, too, have made many people embrace a holistic worldview, which a number of new religions advocate. The ethical aspects of biotechnology and the use of nuclear energy are also among the concerns that some religious sects are beginning to address. Environmental protection movements are rediscovering the ecological merit of the ancient Shinto view of the organic relationship between humans and nature.

A Japanese newspaper article of June 2000 reported that some Japanese are breaking away from the traditional Buddhist funerals and are having their ashes returned to nature rather than placed in a graveyard.[5] The article described how the ashes of thirty-six people, including those of eleven Japanese, were launched in a rocket from Vandenberg Air Force Base in California on December 20, 1999, and noted that the funeral company that arranges the "space burial" had been receiving telephone inquiries daily concerning the next rocket launch, scheduled for the spring of 2001. For the Japanese, this option is not only much less expensive than the traditional Buddhist funeral (around $8,500, compared to an average of $25,000) but also because they found it romantic to think of the ashes of their loved ones in the sky. The rocket orbits the earth for eighteen months before it crashes into the atmosphere and burns up. A young woman whose husband's ashes were on the rocket two years after his death was reported as saying that whenever she looked up into the sky, she felt that her husband was present, and that she would like to think that he had "become a star in the sky."

Over the centuries, religious practices have changed and will continue to do so, but the religious sentiments that are expressed in these practices remain timeless.

# Notes

## Chapter 1

1  Quoted in Luis Frois, *Historia de Iapam*, trans. into Japanese by Matsuda Goichi and Kawasaki Momota, *Nihonshi* [A History of Japan], (Tokyo: Chuokoronsha, 1981): 3: 285.

## Chapter 2

1  W. G. Aston, trans., *Nihongi, Chronicles of Japan from the Earliest Times to A.D. 697* (Rutland, VT: Charles Tuttle, 1985): 2:106.

2  R. Tsunoda, *et al.* ed., *Sources of Japanese Tradition* (New York and London: Columbia University Press, 1971): 23–24.

3  J. Kitagawa, *Religion in Japanese History* (New York and London: Columbia University Press, 1966): 13.

4  *Ibid*: 12.

5  *Ibid*: 7.

6  *Ibid*: 8.

7  *Ibid*.

8  *Ibid*.

9  See Yasumoto Biten, *Himiko no nazo* (*Mysteries Surrounding Himiko*) (Tokyo: Kodansha, 1988).

10  Some scholars have proposed that because the compilation of these records was ordered by Emperor Tenmu (r. 673–86) in order to give legitimacy to the imperial family, the myths were heavily manipulated by the compilers. Others argue that although this may well have been the case, ancient folklore and myths are woven into these official Shinto myths and can give us clues as to the ancient Japanese worldview and beliefs.

11  For the accounts of the "gods," see Aston, *Nihongi*, 1:1–108, and B. H. Chamberlain, trans., *The Kojiki, Records of Ancient Matters* (Rutland, VT, and Tokyo: Charles Tuttle, 1981): 15–159.

12  According to the *Records of Ancient Matters*, five single gods were followed by six generations of gods as couples (male and female), and Izanagi and Izanami are considered the "seventh generation" of the couple-gods; according to the *Chronicles of Japan*, three single gods were followed by three couples, and Izanagi and Izanami are the seventh generation, counting from the first single god.

13  Modern scholarship proves this date to be historically untenable.

14  Aston, *Nihongi*: 1:176.

15  This view is propounded by Yanagida Kunio and other ethnographers. Studies of religious practices on Okinawa have also focused on traditional divisions between the female, who tended to the spiritual world, and the male, who tended to the political realm. For a detailed discussion of the imperial princess priestesshood, see M. Yusa, "Women in Shinto: Images Remembered," in Arvind Sharma, ed., *Religion and Women* (Albany, NY: State University of New York Press, 1994): 93–119.

16  Originally, the cycle was every nineteen years.

## Chapter 3

1  Just when the Buddha actually lived is disputed among scholars. Traditional dates are 623/624–543/544 B.C.E., but critical scholarship places him 463–383 B.C.E.

2  See Carol Anderson, *Pain and Its Ending* (Richmond, Surrey, 1999). This doctrine, although central to the Theravada tradition, was a later interpolation into the oldest layer of the Buddhist canon.

3  Aston, *Nihongi*: 2:65–66.

4  *Ibid*: 2:65–67.

5  Tamura Encho, *Kodai chosen-bukkyo to nihon-bukkyo* (*Ancient Korean Buddhism and Japanese Buddhism*)

(Tokyo: Yoshikawa Kobunkan, 1980): 66.

6 *Ibid*: 39 and 43–44.

7 For the Seventeen-Article Constitution see Tsunoda, *Sources of Japanese Tradition*: 51–53.

8 Aston, *Nihongi*: 2:148–49. The translation is slightly altered.

9 *Ibid*: 2:122.

10 Tamura, *Kodai chosen-bukkyo to nihon-bukkyo*: 170.

11 Tsunoda, *Sources of Japanese Tradition*: 97.

12 *Ibid*: 99.

13 Leon Hurvitz, *Scripture of the Lotus Blossom of the Fine Dharma* (New York: Columbia University Press, 1976): 298.

14 Sekiguchi Shindai, *Mahashikan* (A comprehensive instruction on cessation and contemplation) (Tokyo: Iwanami Shoten, 1983): 1:261–311.

15 Tsunoda, *Sources of Japanese Tradition*: 143–44.

16 Kitagawa, *Religion in Japanese History*: 39.

17 For a case study see H. B. Earhart, *A Religious Study of the Mount Haguro Sect of Shugendo* (Tokyo: Sophia University, 1970).

18 *Majjima-nikaya* (sutra 115).

19 Iwamoto Yutaka, *Bukkyo nyumon* (*An introduction to Buddhism*) (Tokyo: Chuokoronsha, 1964): 115.

## Chapter 4

1 The Buddha lamented that his teachings would gradually decline. The first period, the "period of genuine teachings," would be followed by the "period of diluted teachings," and finally by the "period of the end of teachings," which would last for the next 10,000 years.

2 Scriptural sources that supported their view included the *Lotus Sutra*, which contains the episode of the eight-year-old daughter of a Naga king attaining Buddhahood, and the *Greater Pure Land Sutra*, in which Amida pledged that no woman would be denied salvation.

3 Ohashi Shun'no, *Senchaku hongan nenbutsu-shu* (Honen's Collection of Passages on the Original Vow of Amida in Which the Nenbutsu is Chosen

above All Other Ways of Achieving Rebirth) (Tokyo: Iwanami Shoten, 1999): 209–10.

4 Mizu Shobo, ed., *Hachinin no soshitachi* (Eight Founders) (Tokyo: Mizu Shobo, 1980): 120.

5 Tsunoda, *Sources of Japanese Tradition*: 208.

6 *Ibid*: 210.

7 Tsunoda, *Sources of Japanese Tradition*: 244–46. In his *Drink Tea and Prolong Life* (*Kissa yojo-ki*), Eisai claimed that tea strengthens one's heart, and since the healthy heart regulates all the other organs, if one drinks plenty of tea, "one's energy and spirits will be restored to full strength." We may mention here that modern scientists suspect that green tea helps ward off cancer.

8 *Ibid*: 242–43.

9 Dogen, *A Primer of Soto Zen*, trans. by R. Masunaga, (Honolulu: The University Press of Hawaii, 1978): 27–28 *et passim*.

10 This is the view advanced by Martin Collcutt. On the Chinese Chan masters also see Martin Collcutt, *Five Mountains, The Rinzai Zen Monastic Institution in Medieval Japan* (Cambridge, MA, and London: Harvard University Press, 1981).

11 Daito also established a nunnery, Myokakuji (no longer in existence), where women could undergo Zen training.

12 Ohashi Shun'no, ed., *Ippen shonin goroku* (*Sayings of the Holy Ippen*) (Tokyo: Iwanami Shoten, 1985).

## Chapter 5

1 This idea can be traced back to India and China. Tsunoda, *Sources of Japanese Tradition*: 269.

2 *Ibid*: 270.

3 *Ibid*: 269–70.

4 *Ibid*: 274.

5 "Zo Ise nisho daijingu hoki hongi" ("A precious account of the creation of the two great shrines of Ise"), in Ishida Ichiro, ed., *Shinto shiso-shu* (*Collection of Works on Shinto Thought*) (Tokyo: Chikuma Shobo, 1970): 107–32.

6 Ishida, *Shinto shiso-shu*: 40, 108, and 134.

7 Okada Akio, *et al*, *Nihon no rekishi* (*A History of Japan*) (Tokyo: Yomiuri Shinbunsha, 1959): 6:184–85.

8 *Ibid*, 6:180–84.

9 "Shuron," attributed to Priest Gen'e, reprinted in Kitagawa Tadahiko and Yasuda Akira, ed., *Kyogen-shu* (*Collected Kyogen Plays*) (Tokyo: Shogakukan, 1972): 418–39.

10 *The Pillow Book of Sei Shonagon*, trans. and ed. Ivan Morris (New York and Oxford: Columbia University Press, 1991): 53.

11 Muso was the *dharma*-heir of Koho Ken'nichi.

12 Kosai Tsutomu, "Fukanji nidai" ("The second master of the 'Fukanji' temple"), in *Zeami Shinko* (*Revisiting Zeami*) (Tokyo: Wan'ya Shoten, 1980): 3–8.

13 The Jesuit order, established by Ignatius of Loyola as a reaction to the Reformation, was granted full papal recognition in 1543.

14 Letter dated November 5, 1549, reprinted in Georg Schurhammer, *Francis Xavier, His Life, His Times* (Rome: The Jesuit Historical Institute, 1982): 4:82.

15 *Ibid*: 4:154.

16 *Ibid*: 4:224–25.

17 *Ibid*: 4:221.

18 Okada, *Nihon no rekishi*: 7:76.

19 Iwao Seiichi, *Sakoku* (*Nihon no Rekishi*) (*Closure of the Ports: A History of Japan*, vol. 14) (Tokyo: Chuokoronsha, 1971): 81–83.

20 James Murdoch, *A History of Japan* (New York: Frederick Ungar, 1964): vol. 2, part 1, 243.

21 Iwao, *Sakoku*: 77–78.

22 Murdoch, *A History of Japan*: 2.1:288.

23 The *sengu* of 1585 took place after a hiatus of 129 years for the Inner Shrine, due to the severe decline in imperial financial resources. The Outer Shrine was rebuilt in 1563, thanks to a fundraising campaign carried out by a Buddhist nun, Seijun.

## Chapter 6

1 Okada, *Nihon no rekishi*: 8:123–28.

2 Engelbert Kaempfer, *The History of Japan* (Glasgow: James MacLehose, 1906): 2:2.

3 Hirakubo Akira, *Ingen* (Tokyo: Yoshikawa Kobunkan, 1962).

4 In the same year, 1665, the shogunate issued the "Regulations for the Shinto Shrines and Clerics" (*Shosha negi kan'nushi hatto*). They entrusted Shinto rituals related to the imperial court to the aristocratic Shirakawa family, which had traditionally overseen Shinto matters at court. The Yoshida family acquired a monopoly over other Shinto rituals.

5 *S.v.* "Danka seido," "Jusan butsu," *Bukkyo daijiten* (*Dictionary of Buddhism*) (Tokyo: Shogakukan, 1988).

6 Wing-Tsit Chan, trans. and compiled, *A Source Book in Chinese Philosophy* (Princeton, NJ: Princeton University Press, 1963): 588–653.

7 Shimada Kenji, *Shushigaku to Yomeigaku* (Tokyo: Iwanami Shoten, 1993): 28–29.

8 Tsunoda, *Sources of Japanese Tradition*: 351.

9 Okada, *Nihon no rekishi*: 8:36–37.

10 See, for instance, Mary Evelyn Tucker's work on Kaibara Ekiken (Ekken), *Moral and Spiritual Cultivation in Japanese Neo-Confucianism* (Albany, NY: State University of New York Press, 1989).

11 He was appointed "Shinto specialist" of the Shogunate court in 1682.

12 Herman Ooms, *Tokugawa Ideology, Early Constructs, 1570–1680* (Princeton, NJ: Princeton University Press, 1989): 224.

13 *Ibid*: 103 and 222–28.

14 *Ibid*: 231–32.

15 Tsunoda, *Sources of Japanese Tradition*: 585.

16 Matsuo Basho, "The Records of a Weather-exposed Skeleton": Nobuyuki Yuasa, trans., *The Narrow Road to the Deep North and Other Travel Sketches* (Harmondsworth, Middlesex: Penguin Books, 1966): 53–54. Translation slightly altered.

17 Robert Morrell, trans., *Sand and Pebbles* (Albany, NY: State University of New York Press, 1985): 72.

18 Basho, "Prose Poem on the Unreal Dwelling," in Donald Keene, ed., *Anthology of Japanese Literature* (New York: Grove Press, 1955): 374.

19 Okada, *Nihon no rekishi*: 9:106.

20 Tsunoda, *Sources of Japanese*

*Tradition*: 374.

21 See *Women and Wisdom of Japan* (London: John Murray, 1914): 36, 38, and 44. Neither the author's nor the translator's name is given.

22 Inoue Zenjo, *Tokeiji to kakekomi onna* (*The Tokeiji Temple and Women Taking Refuge*) (Tokyo: Yurindo, 1985). For a case study see D. E. Wright, "Severing the Karmic Ties that Bind: The 'Divorce Temple' Mantokuji," *Monumenta Nipponica* 52.3 (1997): 357–80.

23 Miyata Noboru, *Kami no minzokushi* (*Ethnography of Gods*) (Tokyo: Iwanami Shoten, 1979): 81–87.

24 *Ibid*: 9:110–12.

25 Kitagawa, *Religion in Japanese History*: 170.

26 Ishida, *Shinto shiso-shu*: 300.

27 Hirata Atsutane, "The Land of the Gods," in Tsunoda, *Sources of Japanese Tradition*, 544.

28 Okada, *Nihon no rekishi*: 9:112–13.

29 D. T. Suzuki, *Zen and Japanese Culture* (Princeton, NJ: Princeton University Press, 1973): 244 and plate #51.

## Chapter 7

1 Murakami Shigeyoshi, *Kokka Shinto* (*State Shinto*) (Tokyo: Iwanami Shoten, 1991): 70–73.

2 Miyata, *Kami no minzokushi*: 169–82.

3 Kasahara Kazuo, ed., *Nihon shukyoshi* (*A History of Japanese Religions*) (Tokyo: Yamakawa Shuppansha, 1977): 2:264–68.

4 Martin Collcutt, "Buddhism: The Threat of Eradication," in Marius B. Jansen and Gilbert Rozman, eds, *Japan in Transition: From Tokugawa to Meiji* (Princeton, NJ: Princeton University Press, 1986): 148–49 *et passim*.

5 J. E. Ketelaar, *Of Heretics and Martyrs in Meiji Japan* (Princeton, NJ: Princeton University Press, 1990).

6 Fujitani Toshio and Naoki Kojiro, *Ise Jingu* (Tokyo: San'itsu Shobo, 1960): 169–70.

7 *Ibid*: 170.

8 W. E. Griffiths, *Verbeck of Japan, A Citizen of No Country* (New York, Chicago, Toronto: Fleming H. Revell, 1900): 264.

9 Murakami, *Kokka Shinto*: 17–19.

10 This document was largely drawn by Motoda Nagazane (or Eifu), a devout Confucian-royalist.

11 Dohi Akio, *Nihon Purotesutanto Kirisutokyoshi* (*History of Japanese Protestantism*) (Tokyo: Shinkyo Shuppansha, 1980): 43.

12 Murakami, *Kokka Shinto*: 201.

13 Aston, *Nihongi*: 1:131.

14 W. P. Woodard, *The Allied Occupation of Japan 1945–1952 and Japanese Religions* (Leiden: E. J. Brill, 1972).

15 *Ibid*: 316.

16 H. N. McFarland, *The Rush Hour of the Gods: A Study of the New Religious Movements in Japan* (New York, Evanston, IL, and London: Harper & Row, 1967).

17 Kasahara, *Nihon shukyoshi*: 2: 362–63.

18 Shimazono Susumu, "New Religious Movements," in M. R. Mullins, Shimazono, and P. L. Swanson, eds, *Religion & Society in Modern Japan: Selected Readings* (Fremont, CA: Asian Humanities Press, 1993): 222.

19 McFarland, *The Rush Hour of the Gods*: 123–44.

20 Shimazono, "New Religious Movements": 227. In 2000 Soka Gakkai reported its membership as being 8,200,000 households.

21 Kasahara, *Nihon shukyoshi*: 2:397.

22 *Ibid*: 2:332–33.

## Chapter 8

1 Shimazono, "New Religious Movements": 227–28.

2 Kanariya no kai, ed., *Oum o yameta watakushitachi* (*We Who Quit Aum Shinrikyo*) (Tokyo: Iwanami Shoten, 2000).

3 R. J. Lifton, *Destroying the World to Save It: Aum Shinrikyo, Apocalyptic Violence, and the New Global Terrorism* (New York: Henry Holt, 1999): 236–37.

4 For a concise coverage of this debate see "Articles, Review Essays, and Response on the Theme of 'Abortion and Mizuko kuyo in Japan,'" *Journal of the American Academy of Religion*, 67.4 (December 1999): 737–823.

5 "New funerals emerging: Burials at sea and space," *Asahi Evening News*, 29 June 2000: 1–2.

# Glossary

**Amaterasu** The great sun goddess and imperial ancestor. The Inner Shrine at Ise is dedicated to her.

**Amida Buddha** Amitābha Buddha in Sanskrit; Amida-butsu in Japanese. As Bodhisattva Dharmākara he pledged that should he attain buddhahood he would save every soul who invokes his name in total devotion; he resides in his Western Paradise.

**Bodhisattva, bodhisattva** *Bosatsu* in Japanese; a being who is on his/her way to achieving enlightenment but remains in this world to save others; embodies the **Mahāyāna** ideal of compassion.

**Buddha, buddha** "Awakened One"; *hotoke* in Japanese. **Mahāyāna Buddhism** holds that buddhahood is accessible to all beings. Cf. **Śākyamuni Buddha**.

**Chan** *Zen* in Japanese. Chinese pronunciation of the Sanskrit word *dhyāna*, meaning "meditation."

**chanoyu** "Tea ceremony"; brewing tea became an art form during the Muromachi period, largely under the influence of **Zen** Buddhism.

**Chronicles of Japan** *Nihonshoki* or *Nihongi*; compiled in 720, this work contains the earliest historical records of Japan and of Shinto myths.

**Confucianism** *Jukyō* in Japanese; one of the ancient Chinese philosophical schools, featuring the moral teachings of Confucius (Kōshi in Japanese). Its dominant note is the cultivation of "humanity" (*ren* in Chinese; *jin* in Japanese). Mencius (Mōshi in Japanese) is considered the second sage after Confucius, although the rationalist approach of Xun Zi (Junshi in Japanese) also merits attention. A renewed study of Confucianism gave rise to Neo-Confucianism.

**danka system** Implemented during the Edo period; each family was obliged to be affiliated with a Buddhist temple as its sponsor.

**daigongen** *See* **gongen.**

**daimyōjin** *See* **myōjin.**

**Daoism** *Dōkyō* in Japanese; Chinese philosophical tradition, initially based on the ideas of Lao Zi (Rōshi in Japanese) and Zhuang Zi (Sōshi in Japanese). In both its philosophical and its religious forms (which practiced the quest for longevity and the attainment of supernatural power), it richly informed Japanese popular religions, poetry, and literature.

**dōsojin** Deities encountered in folk religions and said to guard the borders of each village.

**esoteric Buddhism** Largely associated with the **Shingon** and **Tendai** sects. It refers to the "hidden" doctrines, which must be learned directly from the teacher, as opposed to the exoteric doctrines, which are "open" and can be learned from texts and *sūtras*.

**essence-manifestation theory** "Honji-suijaku"; the theory advocated by Buddhists that **Buddha** was the essence and Shinto deities the manifestations of that essence.

**five hindrances, threefold submission** *Goshō-sanshō* in Japanese; a misogynistic justification of women's alleged spiritual inferiority and need to submit to male authority.

**Five Mountain culture** During the Kamakura and Muromachi periods, major **Zen** temples—five in Kamakura, and five (or more) in Kyoto—were designated by the shogunate as the cultural centers; they contributed to the blossoming of the Zen-inspired Japanese culture.

**Flower Garland Sūtra** *Avatamsaka sūtra* in Sanskrit; *Kegon-kyō* in Japanese. The Chinese Huayan school and the Japanese Kegon school are based on the teachings of this *sūtra*.

**genze riyaku** "This-worldly profit"; a dominant trait of popular Japanese religious beliefs.

**Golden Light Sūtra** *Suvarna-prabhāsa sūtra* in Sanskrit; *Konkōmyō-saishōō-kyō* or *Konkōmyō-kyō* in Japanese. A **Mahāyāna sūtra**, one of whose themes is benevolent kingship as a way of governing the country.

**gongen, daigongen** Incarnation, or *avatar*, of the **Buddha** essence in the form of a *kami* deity. "Daigongen" means the "great incarnation."

**Greater Pure Land Sūtra** *See* **Pure Land Sūtra**.

**Hīnayāna Buddhism** Literally, "Small Vehicle." A pejorative term coined by the followers of **Mahāyāna**, the "Great Vehicle." A preferred term is "**Theravāda**," the "way of the Elders."

**Imperial Rescript on Education** "Kyōiku chokugo" (1890), an official rescript confirming the emperor's divine status; it helped pave the way for modern Japanese ultranationalism.

**Ise** The town where the shrine dedicated to the sun goddess **Amaterasu** is located; a sacred place, where the winds from the sea blow pleasantly as the ocean waves wash ashore.

**Ise *mairi*** Popular practice of pilgrimage to the **Ise** Shrine.

**Izanagi** Literally, "he who invites"; together with **Izanami**, this *kami* deity created the islands of Japan.

**Izanami** Literally, "she who invites"; together with **Izanagi**, this *kami* deity created the islands of Japan.

**Izumo** The area occupied by a powerful clan which opposed the imperial family; the Izumo Shrine enshrines the deity Ōkuninushi, a descendant of **Susanoo**.

***jingūji*** Buddhist temples erected in the compounds of Shinto shrines, where the *kami* deities underwent Buddhist practice to attain enlightenment; a product of the Buddhists' attempt to incorporate Shinto into their fold.

**Jinja Shinto** "Shrine Shinto"; a euphemism for the state-imposed worship of Shinto, which became a spiritual force behind Japanese ultranationalism prior to and during World War II.

**Jinmu** The first legendary emperor of Japan; according to Shinto myth, he founded the nation of Japan in the year 660 B.C.E.

***jiriki*** Literally, "self-power"; reliance on one's own effort to achieve religious salvation. Cf. *tariki*.

**Ji-shū** The "Timely" sect, established by Ippen; features the practice of chanting *nenbutsu*.

**Jizō** Kshitigarbha in Sanskrit. **Bodhisattva** with the power to save beings from condemnation to hell; he is especially worshipped as the protector of children.

**Jōdo Shin-shū** "True Pure Land" sect; it grew out of the teachings of Shinran and emphasizes utter reliance on the saving grace of **Amida Buddha**.

**Jōdo-shū** "Pure Land" sect, founded by Hōnen; emphasizes the sustained single-minded chanting of *nenbutsu*.

***kakure kirishitan*** "Crypto-Christians"; refers to Japanese Christians who went underground for over 200 years during the Edo period, when their religion was banned.

***kami*** "God(s)," "deity," or "deities"; the main objects of worship in ancient Shinto practice. The *kami* may be the spirits residing in natural objects, personified deities, or deified persons; *kami* spirits are awe-inspiring and can be benevolent or malevolent.

***kamikaze*** Or *kamkaze*, or *shinpū*; literally, "divine wind." Originally an adjective used to describe the coast of **Ise**. Following the Mongol invasion it became a symbol of national invincibility, and during World War II it was adopted as the name of the suicide mission bombers.

**Kan'non** **Bodhisattva** of mercy, second in rank to **Amida Buddha**. An Indian bodhisattva, Avalokiteśvara, was transfigured into a goddess of mercy in China and Japan. (Kan'non is the semantic transcription of the Sanscrit word for Avalokiteśvara.) Her cult resembles that of the Virgin Mary in the Catholic tradition.

***kekkai*** The Indian monastic Buddhist practice of drawing invisible borders to designate a consecrated place, into which outsiders are forbidden to enter. Japanese monastic Buddhists adopted this practice.

***kōan*** A problem to meditate and solve; a device often used in **Zen** Buddhism to bring about a breakthrough for students. It challenges the epistemological subject–object dichotomy, and brings the issues "home" to our physical reality, which, as Zen insists, is an integral part of our intellectual understanding.

***Kogaku*** "Ancient Learning"; the movement of "return to Confucius and Mencius" advocated by a group of Japanese **Confucian** scholars during the Edo period.

**Kokin-shū**   Kokin Poetry Collection; a collection of poems compiled in 905. The collection reveals aristocratic, refined sentiments, which later came to be described as "effeminate and delicate."

**Kokka Shinto**   State Shinto; Shinto elevated to the status of a national religion after the Meiji Restoration of 1868. Cf. **Jinja Shinto**.

**Kokugaku**   "Native Learning," developed during the Edo period among scholars who asserted the uniqueness of ancient Japanese spirituality. As an ideology it formed the backbone of modern Japanese ultranationalism.

**kuyō**   Comes from the Hindu practice of "pūjā"; in the Japanese context, it means to offer a memorial service for the dead.

**kyōgen**   A medieval theatre genre of farcical comedy, performed in between serious **noh** plays.

**Lotus Sūtra**   *Saddharma-pundarīka sūtra* in Sanskrit; *Myōhōrenge-kyō* or *Hoke-kyō* in Japanese; the most influential Mahāyāna Buddhist scripture, which gave rise to various Japanese Buddhist sects.

**Mahāyāna Buddhism**   A strand of Buddhism that grew out of lay Buddhist movements in India around the first century C.E.; it focuses on **bodhisattva** practices, which will bring universal salvation to all sentient beings. Cf. **Hīnayāna Buddhism, Theravāda Buddhism,** and **Vajrayāna Buddhism**.

**mandala**   Depictions of the universe using symbolic iconic pictorial devices; used in **esoteric Buddhist** practices. The twofold diamond mandala and womb mandala aid the meditator to advance in his or her spiritual awakening.

**Man'yō-shū**   The oldest known collection of Japanese poems (*waka*), compiled around 756. The poems reflect the uncomplicated spirituality of the ancient Japanese people.

**mappō**   The period of the "end of the Buddhist teaching," which follows the periods of "genuine Buddhist teaching" and "diluted Buddhist teaching"—elements of a Buddhist view of history in which the **Buddha**'s teachings are believed to gradually decline.

**matsuri**   A Japanese word for "festival"; related to the following two entries.

**matsuri-goto**   Ancient Japanese word for "politics," meaning to rule the country in accordance with the will of the **kami** deities.

**matsuru**   A verb meaning to "pay proper respect to the **kami** deities," which, in the days of theocracy, was synonymous with taking care of political affairs and religious observances. The word *matsuri* (festival) is derived from this.

**myōjin, daimyōjin**   A Buddhist word referring to Shinto deities in general; it is also a title given to Shinto deities who protect Buddhism. The deity Kariba, who helped Kūkai find the site for his monastery at Mt. Kōya, is called a *myōjin. Daimyōjin* means the "great *myōjin.*"

**Nara Buddhist schools**   Schools of Buddhism that flourished in Nara during the Nara period. Their influence continued throughout history, and temples such as Tōdaiji, Kōfukuji, and Hōryūji still enjoy great prestige to this day.

**nenbutsu**   The devotional act of chanting the mantra "Homage to **Amida Buddha**" (*namu Amida-butsu*).

**Nichiren-shū**   The "Nichiren sect" or "Lotus sect," founded by Nichiren, who upheld the importance of self-improvement and steadfast faith in the Eternal **Buddha** as preached in the **Lotus Sūtra**.

**Ninigi**   A grandson of **Amaterasu**, and the grandfather of the emperor **Jinmu**. His name in full is "Ame nigishi kuni nigishi amatsu hidaka hiko ho no ninigi," which means the "Prince bounty," who shines high in heaven and is prosperous in heaven and on earth."

**noh**   A Japanese theatre form that developed during the Muromachi period. Zeami injected the mental and spiritual elements of **Zen** Buddhism into this art.

**Ōbaku-shū**   A **Zen** sect founded by the Chinese **Chan** master, Ingen; he transmitted the practice, which combines **nenbutsu** and **zazen**.

**okagemairi**   "Thanksgiving visit" to the **Ise** Shrine; this became a periodic nationwide pilgrimage during the Edo period.

**Onmyōdō**   Literally, "Yin–Yang practice"; a Japanese adaptation of Chinese practices of divination, geomancy (i.e. *fengshui*), fortune-telling, astronomy, etc., which were further blended with ancient native Japanese sensibilities such as purity, defilement, mountain worship, asceticism, and so forth.

*onryō*   Or *goryō*; an angry spirit that may possess people, or wreak havoc on those against whom the spirit holds grudges. Festivals such as the Gion Festival were originally conceived in order to pacify such spirits.

**Pillow Book, The**   A collection of essays written by Lady Sei Shōnagon (c. 968– c. 1025) between 994 and 1000. It portrays the lives of aristocrats of the Heian period.

**Primal Shinto**   Also known as "Yuiitsu Shinto" or "Yoshida Shinto." It maintains that Shinto has its own unique worldview and theology.

**Pure Land**   The Buddhist term for "paradise." Every **Buddha** has his own "pure land," into which devotees are reborn. The most famous is **Amida's** "Western Paradise."

**Pure Land Sūtra (Greater Sutra)**   *Sukhavati-vyūha sūtra* in Sanskrit, or *Description of the Land of Bliss*; *Daimuryōju-kyō* in Japanese. *Sūtra* describing the forty-eight vows of Bodhisattva Dharmākara (who later became **Amida Buddha**); it is especially important for followers of the True Pure Land sect. Cf. *Sūtra on the Visualisation of the Pure Land*.

**Queen Shrimala Sutra**   *Śrīmālādevī simhanāda sūtra* in Sanskrit; *Shōman-gyō* in Japanese. A *sūtra* that preaches to court ladies the merits of religious practice as lay followers.

**Records of Ancient Matters**   *Kojiki*; compiled in 712, this contains the earliest mytho-historical accounts of Japan.

**Rinzai-shū**   A Zen sect, founded by Eisai. Its historical development owed much to Chinese masters who settled in Japan; its training method uses **kōan** to quicken the awakening of the mind.

**Saigū**   The office of the priestesshood filled by the imperial princesses, who were chosen by divination to serve the sun goddess **Amaterasu** at **Ise**.

**Saiin**   A replica of the office of **Saigū** in Kyoto, established in the ninth century.

*saiō*   Imperial princess who served as the head priestess at **Ise**; she was considered the "august cane" on which **Amaterasu** relied.

**Śākyamuni Buddha**   (Siddhartha Gautama, possibly 463–383 B.C.E.) The historical **Buddha**, who saw in meditation and contemplation the way to *nirvāna*.

**Sanskrit**   The refined ancient Indian language; many **Mahāyāna Buddhist** scriptures are written in Sanskrit or hybrid Sanskrit.

*sengū*   Or *shikinen sengū*; a periodic rebuilding of the shrine buildings at the **Ise** Shrine. Old shrine buildings are dismantled after the new ones are built every twenty years.

*senzo kuyō*   The offering of a memorial service to one's ancestors; an enduring feature of Japanese religious practice. Cf. **kuyō**.

**Shakyamuni Buddha**   See **Śākyamuni Buddha**.

*shinbutsu bunri*   Literally, "separation of Shinto from Buddhism"; a measure implemented in 1868 by traditionalists who were intent on elevating Shinto into the status of a national faith.

*shinbutsu shūgō*   Literally, the "overlapping" or "fusing of Shinto and Buddhism"—a strong feature of Japanese religious practice.

**Shingaku**   "Mind Learning"; a moral practical philosophy for townspeople developed by Ishida Baigan during the Edo period; it infused morality into the world of merchants.

**Shingon-shū**   The Shingon sect, established by Kūkai in the ninth century. "Shingon" means "true word" or "mantra."

*shinkoku*   Literally, "divine country"—the idea that Japan is protected by **kami** deities, and thus is invincible.

**Shugendō**   A religious practice developed out of mountain asceticism. The **esoteric Buddhist** worldview, depicted by the womb **mandala** and diamond mandala, was applied to natural geographic features; incorporating *yin–yang* doctrines, it formed the cosmology of the mountain ascetics. Cf. **yamabushi**.

**Sōtō-shū**   A Japanese **Zen** sect whose origin can be traced back to Dōgen, who emphasized sitting meditation as the central act of Zen practice.

**Susanoo**   A wind god; a younger brother of the sun goddess, **Amaterasu**. According to legend he was banished to **Izumo**, where he became the local hero, and his descendants gave their lands to the imperial family.

*sūtra*   *Kyō* or *o-kyō* in Japanese; generic term for the Buddhist sacred texts. Japanese Buddhists use Chinese translations of sacred texts from Sanskrit, Pāli (another language of India, in which many early Buddhist canons were written), and Tibetan.

**Sūtra on the Visualization of the Pure Land** *Kanmuryōju-kyō* or *Kan-gyō* in Japanese. The Chinese **Pure Land** master, Shandao (Zendō in Japanese), found in this *sūtra* the promise of salvation for anyone who invoked **Amida**'s name by the single-minded practice of *nenbutsu*. Hōnen developed Shandao's teaching further.

**Tale of Genji, The** Novel written shortly after 1000 C.E. by Lady Murasaki Shikibu (973–1014?); it is permeated by a gentle pathos and an emotive reaction to people, things, and events.

**Tale of the Heike, The** A series of stories, which emerged during the thirteenth century, depicting the battle between the Minamoto clan ("Genji") and the Taira clan ("Heike"). The political eminence of the Taira family dramatically collapsed within a couple of decades, and this reinforced the medieval view of the impermanence of all things, which did not spare even "the mightiest and the proudest."

*tariki* Literally, "other power"; reliance on the mercy of **Amida Buddha** by discarding one's own efforts, which are ultimately doomed by self-conceit. Cf. *jiriki*. Some religious thinkers hold that *jiriki* and *tariki* are two sides of the same **Mahāyāna** spirituality, and should not be separated.

**Tendai-shū** Tendai sect, which grew out of the monastic center established by Saichō at Mt. Hiei. It asserts the universal salvation of all sentient beings.

*ten'nō* Literally, "heavenly emperor"; a title given to the Japanese emperor. The "emperor system" (*ten'no-sei*) is based on the claim that the imperial lineage has been transmitted from the "Age of the God" to the present day.

**Theravāda Buddhism** Grew out of early Indian Buddhism, and monastic in orientation. Its followers adhere strictly to the Buddhist precepts. This strand of Buddhism prevails in South Asia. Also known as **Hīnayāna Buddhism**.

**three bodies of Buddha** The "trikāya" doctrine, developed by the Indian **Mahāyāna** Buddhists, which holds that the **Buddha**-essence manifests itself in (1) the historical form (e.g., Śākyamuni

**Buddha**), (2) the recompensing form (e.g., **Amida Buddha**), and (3) the cosmic essence (represented by Mahāvairocana Buddha).

**three (imperial) regalia** Refers to the mirror, the sword, and the curved jewel, all of which have mythological origin and are in the possession of the reigning emperor.

**Toyouke** The goddess of food, agriculture, and natural bounties; she is the deity enshrined at the Outer Shrine of **Ise**.

**Tsukiyomi** The moon god; younger brother of the sun goddess, **Amaterasu**.

**Uzume** Or "Ame no uzume no mikoto," the goddess who sang and danced to entice **Amaterasu** out of the cave; she is sometimes considered the founder of Japanese performing arts.

**Vajrayāna Buddhism** "Diamond Vehicle" Buddhism, an **esoteric Buddhist** practice that developed in northern India from the sixth to seventh centuries; its later developments are known as Tantric Buddhism.

**Vimalakīrti Sūtra** *Vimalakīrti-nirdeśa sūtra* in Sanskrit; *Yuima-gyō* in Japanese. A *sūtra* in which Vimalakīrti, the wise and rich layman, demonstrates ultimate enlightenment, surpassing that of the **bodhisattva** of wisdom, Mañjuśrī, or Monju in Japanese.

**Vinaya** *Ritsu* in Japanese. A school developed around the study of the observance of "precepts," one of the three major pillars of early Indian Buddhism; the other two are meditation and the cultivation of wisdom.

*waka* A generic term for Japanese poetry; its main form is 31-syllable short poems, but longer poems also belong to this genre. The *haiku* grew out of the first three stanzas of *waka*.

**Yakushi Nyorai** Medicine Buddha; Bhaisajya-guru in Sanskrit. The **Buddha** of healing, who has enjoyed enormous popularity among Japanese devotees.

*yamabushi* Mountain ascetics who developed a unique form of practice, known as **Shugendō**.

**zazen** Sitting meditation in a cross-legged "full lotus" or "half-lotus" position; the central element of **Zen** practice.

**Zen** Japanese pronunciation of the Sanskrit word *dhyāna*, meaning "concentration-meditation."

# Pronunciation Guide

This guide gives an accepted pronunciation as simply as possible. Letters are pronounced in the usual manner for English unless otherwise indicated in the following list. Japanese vowels sound very much like those in Latin, Italian, or Spanish.

a is pronounced like *a* in "father"
i is pronounced like *i* in "image"
u is pronounced like *oo* in "cook"
e is pronounced like *e* in "pen"
o is pronounced like *o* in "roster"
n can be a syllable by itself, and be pronounced like *n* in "pen"
tsu is pronounced like *ts* in "its" with the addition of a vowel "u"
chi is pronounced like *che* in "cheese"
cho is pronounced like *cho* in "chocolate"

Each Japanese syllable is a combination of a consonant and a vowel; this renders possible poetic forms, such as haiku, based on the syllable count. Each vowel is considered one syllable (in which a consonant has a "0" value). Therefore, "Saiin" (imperial princess priestess at Kamo) is pronounced "sa-i-i-n" (four syllables). Instead of diphthongs, as in English, Japanese has "double vowels," which are pronounced longer (equivalent of two syllables). For instance, Soto (a Zen sect) is pronounced "so-o-to-o" (four syllables), not "so-to." These double vowels are customarily designated by macrons, and therefore Soto should be written Sōtō. Again, *Man'yo-shu*, the ancient collection of poetry, is pronounced "ma-n-yo-o-shu-u" (six syllables), and should be written as Man'yō-shū. For the sake of simplicity, however, we omitted macrons from the present text (except from the glossary and the period names in the Timeline—for the sake of reference, if the reader is interested). The double consonants, as in "kekkai" (the circumscribed area), are pronounced like Italian double consonants, with a staccato: ke-(k)-ka-i (four "beats" as opposed to three).

Sanskrit ś is transcribed as *sh*, as in Shakyamuni (Śākyamuni in Sanskrit). Sanskrit ca is transcribed as *cha* as in Vairochana (Vairocana in Sanskrit).

Chinese words are written according to the *pinyin* spelling, which is a closer approximation of actual pronunciation. "Tao" in the traditional Wade-Giles system is written "Dao" in *pinyin*.

Japanese names are given in the Japanese order: the family name first, followed by the given name.

# Major Festivals and Holidays

| | | |
|---|---|---|
| **January 1** | New Year's Day (*ganjitsu*) | national holiday |
| **February 3** | Setsubun (crossover between winter and spring, a sort of "Groundhog Day") | |
| **February 11** | Day of Founding of the Nation (*kenkoku kinen no hi*) | national holiday |
| **March 3** | Girls' Day, Festival of Peach Blossoms (*momo no sekku*) | |
| **March 20** | Vernal Equinox Day (*shunbun*) | national holiday |
| **May 3** | Day to Celebrate the Constitution (*kenpo kinenbi*) | national holiday |
| **May 5** | Children's Day, Festival of Irises (*tango no sekku*) | national holiday |
| **May 15** | Aoi matsuri, Hollyhock Festival (in Kyoto) | |
| **2nd Friday through 3rd Sunday of May** | Sanja matsuri (in Tokyo, Asakusa) | |
| **July 7** | Tanabata (Star Festival)—mostly observed in August according to the lunar calendar | |
| **July 15** | Bon (*obon*) (a kind of "All Souls' Day")—mostly observed in August | |
| **July 17–24** | Gion matsuri (in Kyoto) | |
| **August 2–7** | Nebuta matsuri, Parade of illuminated giant-sized papier-mâché figures (in Aomori) | major festivals in northern Japan |
| **August 5–7** | Kanto matsuri, Festival of Lanterns hung on tall poles (in Akita) | |
| **August 6–8** | Tanabata, Star Festival (in Sendai) | |
| **August 12–17** | Bon (see July 15) | |
| **September 23** | Autumn Equinox Day (*shubun no hi*) | national holiday |
| **October 9** | Takayama matsuri (Takayama, Nagano Prefecture) | |
| **November 3** | Culture Day (birthday of the Meiji emperor) (*bunka no hi*) | national holiday |
| **November 23** | Thanksgiving Day (*kinro kansha no hi*) | national holiday |
| **December 23** | Emperor Akihito's Birthday (*ten'no tan'jobi*) | national holiday |
| **December 31** | New Year's Eve (*oomisoka*) | |

*Note*: Only major festivals are listed above. Practically every city, town, and village has its own festival (*matsuri*). National holidays not listed include the "Day to Celebrate the Coming of Age" (*seijin no hi*, second Monday of January), the "Day of Green" (*midori no hi*, birthday of the former emperor Hirohito, April 29), the "People's Day Off" (*kokumin no kyujitsu*, May 4), the "Day of the Sea" (*umi no hi*, July 20), the "Day to Respect the Senior Citizens" (*keiro no hi*, September 15), and the "Day of Physical Exercises" (*taiiku no hi, hi*, second Monday of October).

# Suggested Further Reading

## BOOKS

M. ANESAKI, *History of Japanese Religion* (London: Kegan Paul, 1930; reprint, 1963, Tokyo: Tuttle).
As the pioneer of Japanese religious studies, Anesaki wrote extensively on Japanese religions. His description of the Meiji spiritual movements is of special interest.

P. K. R. ARAI, *Women Living Zen* (New York, Oxford: Oxford University Press, 1999).
Field research conducted at a nunnery of the Soto Zen sect in Japan; it opens up a new dimension in the subject of religion and women.

W. G. ASTON, trans., *Nihongi, Chronicles of Japan from the Earliest Times to A.D. 697* (Rutland, VT: Charles Tuttle, 1985).
One of the two primary sources of Shinto myths and the early history of Japan.

B. H. CHAMBERLAIN, trans., *The Kojiki, Records of Ancient Matters* (Rutland, VT and Tokyo: Charles Tuttle, 1981).
With Aston, the other primary source of Shinto myths and early history of Japan.

M. COLLCUTT, *Five Mountains, The Rinzai Zen Monastic Institution in Medieval Japan* (Cambridge, MA and London: Harvard University Press, 1981).
Detailed study of the Chinese masters who came to Japan and laid the foundation for the development of Japanese Zen-related culture.

M. COOPER, *They Came to Japan, An Anthology of European Reports on Japan, 1543–1640* (Berkeley, Los Angeles, and London: University of California Press, 1965).
Accounts of what the European missionaries, tradesmen, and travelers saw in Japan at the time of the first introduction of Christianity in the sixteenth century; rich in detailed observations.

W. B. DAVIS, *Japanese Religion and Society: Paradigms of Structure and Change* (Albany: State University of New York Press, 1992).
This and other works by W. Davis are fine examples of the theoretical, social–scientific study of Japanese religions.

L. HEARN, *Glimpses of Unfamiliar Japan* (Boston and New York: Houghton Mifflin, 1894).
This and other works by Hearn contain folk tales, ghost stories, and descriptions of now-forgotten religious practices; as such they are precious reading.

H. KEYSERLING, *The Travel Diary of a Philosopher* (New York: Harcourt, Brace & Co., 1925).
Part Six comprises Count Keyserling's metaphysical essays on such sacred places as Mt. Koya, Nara, Kyoto, Ise, and Nikko—jewels to be savored.

T. P. KASULIS, *Zen Action, Zen Person* (Honolulu: University Press of Hawaii, 1981).
A unique treatment of Zen from a philosophical perspective. Highly readable, it offers insight into the teachings of Zen.

J. E. KETELAAR, *Of Heretics and Martyrs in Meiji Japan* (Princeton NJ: Princeton University Press, 1990).
A thorough study of the transition that Buddhism underwent in the Meiji period.

J. KITAGAWA, *Religion in Japanese History* (New York and London: Columbia University Press, 1966).
The most complete historical work on Japanese religions.

R. J. LIFTON, *Destroying the World to Save It: Aum Shinrikyo, Apocalyptic Violence, and the New Global Terrorism* (New York: Henry Holt, 1999).
A historical and psychological analysis of the phenomena of Aum Shinrikyo violence and the Oklahoma bombing.

M. R. MULLINS, S. SHIMAZONO, and P. L. SWANSON, eds, *Religion & Society in Modern Japan, Selected Readings* (Fremont, CA: Asian Humanities Press, 1993).
Probably the single most useful sourcebook in English on Japan's "new" and "new-new" religious movements. Bibliography on pp. 229–30 and pp. 301–10 will be useful.

H. Ooms, *Tokugawa Ideology, Early constructs, 1570–1680*. (Princeton, NJ: Princeton University Press, 1989).
Detailed analysis of the Neo-Confucianism of the early Tokugawa period; the study of Yamazaki Ansai is unparalleled.

I. Reader, *Religion in Contemporary Japan* (Honolulu: University of Hawaii Press, 1991).
This work and others by Reader introduced the term, "genze riyaku" (this-worldly profit) into the study of Japanese religions as a viable concept.

G. Schurhammer, *Francis Xavier, His Life, His Times* (Rome: The Jesuit Historical Institute, 1982).
Vol. 4 covers the introduction of Christianity into Japan.

D. T. Suzuki, *Zen and Japanese Culture* (Princeton, NJ: Princeton University Press, 1973).
A classic work on the topic, informative and insightful.

G. Tanabe, Jr., ed., *Religions of Japan in Practice* (Princeton, NJ: Princeton University Press, 1999).
Forty-five essays by leading contemporary scholars of Japanese religions cover a wide terrain, extending from ethical and ritual practices to institutional practices.

R. Tsunoda, W. T. de Bary, and D. Keene, eds, *Sources of Japanese Tradition* (New York and London: Columbia University Press, 1971).
The classic sourcebook in English on Japanese thought.

M. Underwood, E. G. Harrison, W. R. LaFleur, and R. M. Green, "Articles, Review Essay, and Response on the Theme of 'Abortion and Mizuko kuyō in Japan.'" *Journal of the American Academy of Religion* 67.4 (December 1999), 737–823.
These essays offer first-class scholarship on the contemporary issues of abortion in Japan and the religious rituals that surround aborted fetuses.

W. P. Woodard, *The Allied Occupation of Japan 1945–1952 and Japanese Religions* (Leiden: E. J. Brill, 1972).
Rich in first-rate sources; no other book surpasses this one on the topic of postwar Japanese religious reform.

## JOURNALS

Articles published in the following journals are useful: *The Eastern Buddhist*; *Harvard Journal of Asiatic Studies*; *Japan Studies Review* (the journal of the Southern Japan Seminar); *Japanese Journal of Religious Studies*; *Journal of the American Academy of Religion*; *Journal of Asian Studies*; *Journal of Japanese Studies*; *Journal of Religious Studies*; *Monumenta Nipponica*; *Pacific World: Journal of the Institute of Buddhist Studies*; *Philosophy East and West*.

## WEBSITES

*General sites in English*:

Society for the Study of Japanese Religions: http://www.wfu.edu/Organizations/ssjr
Maintained by James L. Ford, Wake Forest University, this site contains useful research information on Japanese religions.

Religious Information Research Center: http://www.rirc.or.jp/data
This site requires some knowledge of written Japanese; it is a "directory" of Japanese religious organizations; very useful.

Japanese Government (The Agency for Cultural Affairs): http://www.mext.go.jp/english/org/index.htm
Contains current statistics on religious affiliation, and the definition of religious juridical persons.

*Other sites in English, specific to sects*:

Association of Shinto Shrines: http://www.jinja.or.jp/english
Konko: http://www.konkokyo.or.jp
Oomoto: http://www.oomoto.or.jp/English/index-en.html
Reiyukai: http://www.reiyukai.or.jp
Rissho Koseikai: http://kosei-kai.or.jp/english/index.html
Soka Gakkai: http://sokagakkai.or.jp
Tenri: http://www.tenrikyo.or.jp
Mt. Koya (Shingon): http://www.koyasan.or.jp; this site has no English text but carries strikingly beautiful photos of Mt. Koya, the appreciation of which requires no knowledge of Japanese.

**Note**: This list is far from exhaustive; try a search engine for others.

# Index

Page numbers in *italics* refer to picture captions.